THE **JONNY WILKINSON** STORY

UNAUTHORISED & UNOFFICIAL

First published in 2004
Second Edition 2007
Copyright © Carlton Books Limited 2004, 2007

A CIP catalogue record for this book
is available from the British Library

ISBN 978-1-84732-081-0

Words:	Iain Spragg & Adrian Clarke
Edited by:	Justyn Barnes & Aubrey Ganguly
Design:	David Hicks & Paul Chattaway
Production:	Lisa Cook
Cover Photo:	Getty Images
Photography:	Empics, Rex Features & Action Images

Printed in Great Britain

Opposite: Jonny in classical pose, following through after striking a
penatly kick towards the posts.
Page 4: Checking his options, Wilkinson looks both ways before deciding
whether to run, pass or kick.
Page 6: A picture of concentration, Jonny waits for the game to restart.

THE **JONNY WILKINSON** STORY
UNAUTHORISED & UNOFFICIAL

Iain Spragg &
Adrian Clarke

CARLTON

CONTENTS

INTRODUCTION

Has England ever had a greater
sportsman than Jonathan Peter
Wilkinson? The man who guided his
country to consecutive Rugby World
Cup finals certainly has few rivals for
the mantle and with his injury-
blighted career finally back on track,
few would bet against him taking
England on another magical World
Cup ride in 2011. This is Jonny's
story so far...

CHAPTER ONE

THE LITTLE BOY WITH ONE BIG DREAM

When Jonny Wilkinson dropped the goal in the dying seconds of extra-time of the World Cup final in Sydney to give England the most dramatic of victories, the 24-year-old's life changed forever. In the split second that it took the ball to sail through the uprights and break Australian hearts, the unassuming fly-half became a national superstar and, whether he liked it or not, his place in sporting folklore was assured.

England had waited so long for an excuse to celebrate their first global sporting triumph since Alf Ramsey led the football team to glory at Wembley in 1966 and Wilkinson was finally the man to provide it. The image of his match-winning kick would be replayed countless times in the days and weeks after the final and already it rivals pictures of Geoff Hurst's hat-trick against Germany in the national consciousness.

But like so many of our true sporting greats, Wilkinson's story is far from one of overnight success. In fact, it was the result of 20 years of dedication, self-sacrifice and hard work which culminated so spectacularly in Sydney's Telstra Stadium, the effortless ease of his strike which claimed the Webb Ellis trophy being the fruit of endless hours spent on the training pitch. Wilkinson was always a man with a plan.

His story began in Frimley, Surrey, on 25 May 1979 when Jonny Peter Wilkinson was born to proud parents Phil and Philippa. He was the second new arrival in the Wilkinson family in the space of two years, following 18 months behind older brother Mark, and the two boys were to become, and remain, firm friends both on and off the pitch (they still share a house together in the north east).

The omens that the younger Wilkinson was to become a star were certainly good. His grandfather, Philip Papworth, had been a professional footballer with Norwich City, while his parents had also shown themselves to be talented players in their respective sports. Phil Wilkinson was a distinguished amateur rugby player with local Surrey club Alton, although unlike his son he was more at home in the bruising world of the forwards than running rings around the opposition in the backs. Philippa Wilkinson had been captain of the Hampshire Ladies squash team when she wasn't working as a secretary at the Foreign and Commonwealth Office in London.

Inevitably, it was not long before the young Wilkinson began to make his own sporting mark. At the tender age of four he began playing mini rugby for his local club Farnham and his incredible journey from junior rugby to the pinnacle of the global game had begun in earnest. Every future superstar, however talented, must still learn his trade and for Wilkinson his education was now in its infancy.

The first major influence on his career was, perhaps predictably, his father Phil who fulfilled both coaching and chauffeuring duties in the early days. But by the age of eight another figure loomed on the horizon in the shape of John Fairley, a man who was to witness first-hand the blossoming of a world-class talent.

"I had just moved into the area and played for Farnham veterans," recalls Fairley. "One day I was watching my lad Alistair playing mini rugby and I saw a guy with wellies, a big jacket and a cigar walking up and down the line, looking a bit frustrated. We started chatting. It was Phil Wilkinson, watching Jonny. Phil wasn't too happy about what was happening in terms of the coaching. It ended up with the pair of us getting involved with coaching the minis."

Both fathers took a Rugby Football Union (RFU) coaching course that was run for parents and while Phil took charge of the year above his son's side, Fairley was to take up the reins of Wilkinson's age group. Fairley is quick to put his input into Wilkinson's development into context but there is little doubt that he played a significant part in the nurturing of an exceptional talent in the all-too-frequent mud baths at Farnham's Wrecclesham Recreation Ground.

"Besides myself, there were probably about a dozen other people who've been involved in Jonny's development," Fairley admits. "In each of us there's a little tinge of pride that one of our boys has reached such heights."

With Wilkinson in the side, Farnham minis began to enjoy great success but, as so often with players who are to become world-class performers, he benefited from having some very talented players around him in his formative years. Rugby, like every team game, is rarely a one-man show.

"Initially, Jonny didn't stand apart," Fairley recalls. "A lad he played with, Andy Holloway, who is scrum-half up at Bedford now, was the first one I noticed. It wasn't until Jonny got to the under-12s, where the game is played more in the shape of senior rugby, that he stood out. He was a quiet lad intent on honing his skills but I remember somebody asking me whether he would ever play for England. I said that he had got all the skills to do it. He always had that innate ability.

"It helped that Jonny played with a group of guys who were very talented. They'd do some fairly prodigious things. We'd get a penalty and I'd be screaming 'Just take the points'. But no, Andy Holloway would take a quick kick, toss it to Jonny, who'd jink and sling that big miss-pass of his for the outside centre to pick up. They had the self-belief to do it."

Fairley was to be part of Wilkinson's rugby life until the future England fly-half left the club at the age of 15, and even in the early years the tell-tale signs of the youngster's now legendary attention to detail, his obsessive quest for perfection, his pre-match nerves and, not least, his outstanding talent were there for all to see.

His first taste of the stage that was to become his second home came at the age of 10 when Farnham Under-11s played at Twickenham in a curtain-raiser for the 1990 Cup final between Bath and Gloucester. It was the same year that his future World Cup-winning team-mate Jason Leonard was to make his senior England debut in Argentina yet here was Wilkinson, not yet a teenager, running out for what was to be the first of many appearances at the spiritual home of rugby.

"I loved every minute of it," Wilkinson said a decade later. "After all, I'd been playing rugby for six years by then!"

In the same year the young Wilkinson was also to experience the glare of the media spotlight for the first time.

"A local BBC TV crew came to film our Under-11s one day," Fairley recalls, "and I suggested that Jonny could drop a goal for them. First, he did it off his left foot. Then he did it off his right foot. The TV people just watched in astonishment."

Little did anyone know that, 13 years later, another television crew would capture another, rather more significant Wilkinson drop goal.

Rugby, however, was not Wilkinson's only talent. Although he was to go on to represent Hampshire schools at both cricket and tennis, it was football that first made the young boy question his commitment to the oval ball. In the same year that he was taking his first tentative steps out on the famous Twickenham pitch, he was also playing football for the first time in his life and judging by his memories of his debut game, rugby's gain was most definitely football's loss."

"I played football for a season when I was 10," Wilkinson said in an interview years later. "Funnily enough the first game I ever played I scored a goal from the halfway line. I didn't have a clue what I was doing. The ball just came to me, so I whacked it and it sailed over the goalie's head and in. I remember thinking at the time 'Yeah, this is easy'."

David Beckham eat your heart out.

Fortunately Wilkinson's dramatic impact with the round ball was not enough to sway him from his first love, rugby. "I started playing rugby when I was four years old," he recalls. "I grew up with a rugby ball rather than a football. My brother Mark was into rugby and we had a very sporty family. So it was just what I knew from a young age and I decided to stick with it. I only played football for a year and it was mainly a social thing. The thing I liked most about rugby was when you get that whole team togetherness coming through against all the pressure of winning a big game. There's no better feeling than having everyone there to share it with. That to me has always been the most prominent thing in rugby because there are quite a few hard-hitting tackles. And you learn how to make friends who you get to know very closely."

At this time, Wilkinson also realised what he desperately wanted more than anything else was to play for England. It was this heartfelt conviction, along with his innate talent, that was to ultimately see him scale the rugby heights. Few people, perhaps even the man himself, could have realised then just how far the precocious 10-year-old would progress over the years that followed but what was abundantly clear was that Wilkinson lacked neither vision nor ambition.

"It was always my dream to play for England," admitted Wilkinson in the build-up to the World Cup in Australia. "When I was 10 or 11, I thought, 'That's what I want to do'. I wrote it down on a piece of paper, kept referring back to it and making sure I did as much as I could to keep to that path. I was tiny for my age then and I could be trouble because I was never satisfied, always too competitive whether it was inside or outside the house."

This now trademark competitiveness was to quickly surface when Wilkinson made the transition from junior to secondary education and he found himself at the rugby-loving Pierrepont School in Surrey. Very quickly his rugby prowess was recognised, although not before a few egos had been thoroughly, if unintentionally, bruised.

Matt Payne was student teacher at the school during Wilkinson's stay and he remembers all too well the young fly-half's arrival on the Pierrepont training pitch. Payne became Wilkinson's first real kicking coach and he still recalls the exact moment when he realised he was working with a very special talent: "We had a goal-kicking competition between the two of us which Jonny won hands down. We both used our right foot. Then, after the embarrassment of losing to a 12-year-old, he asked if I fancied repeating the exercise using my left foot. He'd been kicking with his weaker foot and still beat me!"

At the time Wilkinson was still playing club as well as schools rugby, and it was in the colours of Farnham that John Fairley noticed both his appetite for the physical side of the game and a tendency to worry before a big match. Among the many newspaper cuttings Fairley has kept from his Farnham days, one in particular hints at the fearsome reputation Wilkinson was to earn as one of the international game's fiercest tacklers. It refers to a tackle on a gigantic opposition Number 8 in an Under-13s final and waxes lyrical on how Wilkinson, in those days still little more than skin and bones, had driven the bigger boy back.

"Even then he just used to fly in and hit people very hard," recalls Fairley. "He was always confronting boys twice his size."

Another of Fairley's anecdotes illustrates perfectly how his prodigy was always prone to bouts of self-doubt despite his obvious talent. Wilkinson himself now readily admits he is always "obscenely nervous" before games (he is now famous for his furrowed, anxious brow before kick-off) and it was all too obvious to Fairley that the star-in-the-making found it difficult to relax before a game.

"I remember one day we travelled down on the bus to play Llanelli Under-15s," Fairley says. "He was a bag of nerves all the way down. I mean, he was ashen, he barely said a word for the entire journey. I just thought to myself, 'Jonny, you've got such an immense amount of talent. If I had that, I wouldn't be nervous about playing anyone.'"

However those nerves, along with his conviction that practice makes perfect, were to stand Wilkinson and England in good stead in the years that followed.

Top: Young Jonny (he's the tiny guy in front of the flag) playing for Farnham Under-7s.
Below: Lining up with Farnham Under-13s (front row, third from right).

CHAPTER TWO

THE KID THEY CALLED GOD

If Wilkinson's obvious promise and ambition had been identified and nurtured at Farnham, and subsequently Pierrepont, it was when he moved to Lords Wandsworth College, near Basingstoke in Hampshire, at the age of 14 that his phenomenal rise up the ranks really began to gather pace.

The school was a hotbed of rugby and it provided the young Wilkinson with the stage he needed to push his claim for international recognition and a career in the still embryonic professional game.

In many ways, nothing changed for Wilkinson at Lord Wandsworth. He continued to play with a focus that both amazed and inspired team-mates and coaches alike. As each day and week passed, the boy who was rapidly becoming a man looked more and more like a future England player. The unflinching dedication to his sport, which had begun as a toddler at home as he worked on his technique by kicking toilet rolls around the living room, intensified.

The first XV coach at Wandsworth at the time was Alan Dyson and he, like many before and after him, was struck by his young charge's unwavering commitment: "Jonny was always out on the field practising his kicking. He'd even come down in the school holidays. He was always something else when it came to his focus and concentration."

It is an almost obsessive frame of mind that Wilkinson readily admits to these days: "Once, when I was at school as a teenager, I just couldn't seem to get my place-kicking right. It must have been 7.30 in the morning and I went out with a bag of balls. The next thing I knew it was 12.30. I drove my parents mad as a kid!"

On another occasion, even five hours of practice couldn't satisfy the budding England star.

"I'd spent five hours kicking balls," he says.

"Mum told me to come home but I was upset because I hadn't got where I wanted to be with my kicking. She then sat in the car for another hour-and-a-half while I got it right!"

Legend has it that Wilkinson was given his own key to the school sports hall so that he could hone his skills whenever the mood took him – which, of course, was more often than not. But his search for perfection left him with little time for other interests. A Wandsworth contemporary, Duncan White, remembers: "Girls joined the school in the sixth form: Jonny was always fancied, but he never had any serious relationships."

His dedication soon earned him the nickname 'God' at Wandsworth, but it was the recognition of the junior England selectors that he truly craved. He didn't have to wait long for it to come. In 1997, 16-year-old Jonny pulled on the famous white shirt for the first time when he was called up by England Under-18s. With Wilkinson in the line-up, England were dominant, beating Ireland, Scotland and France, and only Wales stood between them a third Grand Slam in four seasons.

The Wales game, played in April at Narberth, proved to be another defining moment in Wilkinson's career. Wales had not beaten their England counterparts for four years but on home soil level at 7–7 at half-time, it seemed they were on the verge of ending the losing sequence. In fact, the Welsh surged into the lead after the break and despite a second try of the match from Wilkinson's future full England team-mate Mike Tindall, the visitors found themselves trailing 17–15 with the match in second-half injury time. Cue Wilkinson, who unleashed a monstrous drop goal that sailed through the posts to give England a dramatic, Grand Slam-clinching 18–17 victory.

Top: Jonny (front row, fifth from right) gears up to play for Farnham Under-13s.
Below: 10-year-old Jonny plays at Twickenham for the first time in a curtain-raiser for the 1990 Cup final between Bath and Gloucester.

"Jonny hit the drop goal and it was a cracker from about 45 yards out," recalls the then England Under-18s coach Geoff Wappett. "The referee that day admitted later that he didn't actually see the ball go over the posts because of the bright sun, but he awarded it when a Welsh fan behind the posts started swearing!" Tindall, however, has a slightly different memory of the event: "It was definitely a harder drop goal than the one Jonny kicked in Sydney. It was at least 40 yards out. As the ball went over, the Welsh full-back swore, so the referee realised it was on target."

Whatever the referee's reasons, Wilkinson had undeniably arrived on the England scene. But it was from the midfield alongside Tindall rather than the Number 10 berth that he broke Welsh hearts.

"A guy called Jamie Lofthouse was our first-choice fly-half then," reveals Wappett, "but I really wanted him and Jonny to play in the same side. So I played Wilko at Number 12. He was always a fly-half but at that stage Lofthouse was probably slightly more mature when the pressure was on.

After his match-winning performance against Wales, Wilkinson's selection for the Under-21s tour to Australia that summer was a mere formality and England continued to sweep all before them. The team won all eight of their matches on the tour, culminating in a superb 38–20 victory over their junior Wallaby counterparts in North Sydney. They scored 88 tries in the process but it was one of eight that they conceded on the trip that highlighted exactly what makes Wilkinson tick. As Mick Cleary wrote in the *Daily Telegraph* two years after the record-breaking tour: "England thumped a New South Wales team by over 70 points. They conceded just one try, the result of a fluffed tackle. After the match one player sat distraught in the changing room. It was he who had missed the tackle. Jonny Wilkinson was that player."

Wappett remembers: "I went over at the final whistle to congratulate him on a great performance. He was having none of it. He'd made a mistake and he was furious with himself."

Wilkinson concedes he still finds it difficult to take pleasure from a victory if he feels his own performance hasn't met his own exacting standards.

"It does bother me," he said in an interview in 2001. "Rugby is a team game, so you always try and play well for the team. But for myself, I like to feel each time I play I have done something better or managed to be a little bit wiser because I have learned from my mistakes. I know I can't let it affect me during a game though. You have to wait until you are away from the game, on your own, and then you can deal with it."

Wilkinson returned to England after the tour to collect his exam results. Perhaps surprisingly for a lad who had devoted so many hours to his rugby, he did well. A-levels in French, biology and chemistry earned him a place at Durham University to study for a Sport in the Community degree. Fate, however, ensured he never took up his place.

His headmaster at Wandsworth must have had a crystal ball when he wrote in his final year report: "I expect him to be the next England stand-off and to capture the nation's imagination. Go for it, Jonny and the best of luck."

Wilkinson had planned to take a gap year before going to Durham but the intervention of a familiar face from school changed the course of his life and play a huge part in his remarkable rise to become a fully-fledged England star. The face belonged to Steve Bates and the change of direction was to take Wilkinson from his Surrey home to the north east and Newcastle Falcons. Bates was a former England scrum-half and had worked as a coach at Lord Wandsworth. When legendary England fly-half Rob Andrew was appointed Director of Rugby at Newcastle, he was soon on the phone to his former Wasps and England team-mate Bates, who agreed to become the Falcons coach. The wheels were in motion.

One of the first things Bates did when he got to Newcastle was to rave (not for the first time) about Wilkinson's potential. Andrew, who at the time was still England's all-time record points scorer, was keen to see what all the fuss was about and Wilkinson was soon on his way up north. The apprentice was about to meet the master and the man who would become perhaps his greatest mentor.

Top: Slotting another conversion between the posts for Farnham Under-18s.
Below: Ready for action at Twickenham in 1990.

CHAPTER THREE

MEET THE NEW ROB ANDREW

Although they were at opposite ends of their respective playing careers when first united, Rob Andrew and Jonny Wilkinson hit it off instantly at Kingston Park and it was to be the beginning of a partnership that was to benefit both the Newcastle Falcons and, very soon, England.

The pair were almost carbon copies of one another in both temperament and talent. Andrew quickly realised he had his hands on a beautiful, if still rough diamond. Wilkinson couldn't have chosen a better role model at this crucial stage of his career.

It is easy to forget in the afterglow of England's World Cup triumph that, in his day, Andrew was just as influential a performer in a successful England side as Wilkinson is now, and almost as prolific with the boot at the very highest level.

Born in Richmond, North Yorkshire, Andrew made his full England debut against Romania in 1985 and capped a notable start at international level with 18 points. The triple Cambridge Blue had arrived in style and, with only the occasional interruption, became fixture in the England set-up for the next 12 years.

However, it was not until 1994 that he became England's first-choice place kicker and began to rack up the points in earnest – including a then world record 30 against Canada in December that year. In 1989, he was selected for the British Lions tour to Australia and although the coaching team opted for Scotland's Craig Chalmers at fly-half for the first Test against the Wallabies, Andrew fought his way back into contention for the remaining two Tests as the Lions completed a famous 2–1 series victory. Grand Slam triumphs with England in 1991 – the same year that England were beaten in the World Cup final at Twickenham by Australia – 1992 and 1995 were to follow and he was also a member of the 1993 Lions squad that were beaten 2–1 in New Zealand in 1993.

Ironically, however, the defining moment of Andrew's own career came in the shape of a World Cup drop goal against Australia. The World Cup in question was in South Africa in 1995 and the game against the Wallabies was a quarter-final clash. England were bent on revenge for their defeat in the final four years previously but, after a titanic struggle in Cape Town and with time running out, the scores were tied at 22–22. Cue Andrew and his lethal right boot.

England won a crucial line-out, the ball was fed to the England Number 10 and he unleashed a long-range drop goal which sailed through the posts. England had avenged their Twickenham heartache and Andrew was a national hero. Sounds familiar?

Sadly, England were to fall to New Zealand in the semi-final a week later but Andrew had once again proved his worth when England needed him.

In the wake of England's World Cup exit, Andrew quit London and his long-term club Wasps to become Newcastle's player-coach. Two years later, Wilkinson made the same journey north east.

"At first I thought of it almost like a gap year," Wilkinson admit later after turning his back on Surrey. "But I soon realised that to keep at that level I had to give my whole time to it."

Just how in awe of his new boss Wilkinson was remains a mystery (although he was later to admit in an interview that he would "watch England as a kid and I would go straight out and practice my kicking because I dreamed of being the next Rob Andrew"), but it is evident that Andrew was well aware of the talent he had lured to Kingston Park.

"What impressed me was his true class whether in passing or kicking, or just in his general composure,"

Right: New Falcon Jonny immediately impressed Rob Andrew with his class and composure. Overleaf: Evading the challenges of Leicester's Dave Lougheed and Richard Cockerill.

Andrew said in a later interview. "All the leading clubs wanted to sign him when he left school but we had an inside track because of the Steve Bates connection. When Steve and I were still at Wasps, Steve used to turn up at training raving about 'this kid we have at school'. So when Steve came to Newcastle, Jonny was one of the first players we earmarked and because his parents knew and trusted Steve, we managed to persuade him to join us."

Bates remembers Wilkinson's arrival at Newcastle as an unassuming teenager vividly: "When he first came to Newcastle and came into professional rugby he was very shy, nervous and very self-critical of his own performance. I've known him since he was 16, and he has always been an exceptionally dedicated player with a huge understanding of the game. He is the first of the true rugby professionals."

However, Wilkinson was not an instant hit at Newcastle. Although he had often played against older and invariably bigger players during his junior days, he was now in competition with seasoned first-teamers with years of top-level experience. This time there was to be no immediate impression made by the talented but green teenager.

"People talk about my sudden rise but it has all been very gradual really," Wilkinson recalls. "I was on the bench 15 or 16 times for Newcastle before I got on for them. I had to be patient like any young player with no first-team experience and I've just picked things up as I've gone along."

At Newcastle, Wilkinson also joined forces with a man who proved to be a huge influence on his career – England kicking specialist Dave Aldred. Aldred is now recognised as a pioneer in his field but back in 1997, when the two first met at Kingston Park, his art was viewed by many with suspicion. Mercifully, Andrew was not among them. Aldred had spent much of the 1970s in America earning his living in the NFL as a kicker for the Minnesota Vikings. He returned in 1979, keen to return to his rugby union roots, but back in the game's strictly amateur days he was shunned by the establishment who viewed him as a professional.

That all changed when the game embraced professionalism in the wake of the 1995 World Cup and he soon became Andrew's kicking guru. He went on to coach Wales' prolific kicker Neil Jenkins on the successful 1997 Lions Tour of South Africa and the scene was set for him to work his magic on the emerging talent that was Wilkinson.

Aldred can certainly take some credit for the fact that Wilkinson dropped his famous goal in the Telstra Stadium with his right, rather than 'natural' left foot.

"With kicking we do not accept there is a weaker foot," he asserts. "There is simply a different foot. In practice sessions, we used to kick into a net which is placed only a yard away, so the kicker really does learn to kick off both feet. The idea is to make the whole act of, in this case a drop kick, second nature, so that when the fly-half spots an opportunity, instinct just takes over and bang, they go through the kick without worrying about which foot they are using."

Under the guidance of Andrew, Bates and Aldred, Wilkinson settled in and his wait for a first-team start finally came to an end in January 1998 in a Tetley's Bitter Cup fourth-round clash against lower division Exeter. The tie was played in a howling wind, but Wilkinson, who played at centre rather than Number 10, still managed to make a favourable impression.

With the Falcons already 5–0 to the good, the debutant made a superb solo break and then timed his pass to future England full-back Tim Stimpson to perfection. Stimpson rounded off the move with a try and Newcastle were well on their way to a comfortable 34–10 victory.

The near gale conditions made goal-kicking a lottery and Wilkinson missed all three of his place kicks in the first-half. With the game safely in the bag, and Andrew mindful of not over-extending his protégé on his debut, Wilkinson was replaced at the break.

But it had been a valuable learning experience and Wilkinson was about to make the transition from junior phenomenon to senior star. No-one, however, could have predicted the speed of the transformation. Just three months later, the teenager was playing for the full England team.

At Newcastle, Jonny formed a fruitful relationship with England kicking specialist Dave Aldred who is now regarded as a pioneer in the field.

CHAPTER FOUR

HARSH LESSONS DOWN UNDER

Wilkinson made his record-breaking international debut on 4 April 1998, but his first experience of the senior set-up came a fortnight earlier when the England coach Clive Woodward called him into his squad for the Five Nations clash with Scotland at Murrayfield.

England were in the midst of an injury crisis at half-back and, despite the fact that few people outside the north east had heard the name Wilkinson before, Woodward had already received reports of the prodigiously talented Number 10 who had played just 58 minutes of senior rugby. Long-serving England centre Jeremy Guscott hadn't though. The story goes that he thought Wilkinson had won a competition to meet the team when the shy teenager walked into the dressing room for the first time!

It was a bold move by Woodward to name Wilkinson in his squad but he had no doubts that the youngster from Farnham had the temperament to handle the big occasion.

"I think Jonny is ready to play for England now," he told a packed press conference in the build-up to the game. "I'm not interested in the word pressure. Ability overcomes that."

In the end, Wilkinson had to settle for a place on the bench as he watched events unfold at Murrayfield as England blasted their way to a 34–20 win against the Scots.

Jonny had his foot in the England door. Two weeks later he smashed it open.

England's final Five Nations match of the season was against Ireland at Twickenham and Woodward once again named Wilkinson among his substitutes. This time, however, he didn't spend the entire 80 minutes warming the bench. In an ill-tempered and occasionally violent match,

England were always ahead of the Irish and they lead 25–7 at the break. The second-half followed the pattern of the first and, as the final whistle loomed, it seemed Wilkinson was to be denied his first cap once again. But with two minutes on the clock, centre Mike Catt picked up an injury and Wilkinson's moment of destiny had arrived.

"I saw Catty go down," he said after the game, "and I didn't have much time to think about going on. I was warming up beside the pitch and Clive Woodward said, 'You're on the wing'. I didn't have far to run."

For the record, England won the match 35–17, clinching their fourth successive Triple Crown in the process but, sadly for Wilkinson, it was the end of the Five Nations. Although it may have only been a fleeting appearance at Twickenham, in those two minutes Wilkinson became the youngest player, at the age of 18 years and 314 days, to play for England in 71 years. Suddenly he was no longer a talented hopeful, he was a full international player.

The debutant returned to Newcastle on the crest of a wave but his new-found international status still did not guarantee him a place in Rob Andrew's starting line-up as the Falcons clinched the Allied Dunbar Premiership title. He had made incredible strides in his first senior season, culminating in his first cap against Ireland, but by his own admission the 18-year-old still had a lot to learn. And in the summer of 1998 the learning curve suddenly became very steep indeed.

England had scheduled a summer tour for June and July. The trip featured Test matches in Australia, two in New Zealand and a final clash with South Africa in Cape Town. It would have been a severe examination of any side at the best of times but England's preparations for what was to

Jonny warms up before England's Five Nations clash with Scotland... but he'd have to settle for a place on the bench.

become known as the 'Tour of Hell' were blighted by injuries and withdrawals. The team's leading players, who had spent the previous summer in South Africa with the British Lions, pulled out *en masse* after playing 18 months non-stop rugby without a break, and Woodward's plans were thrown into further disarray when a clutch of other players broke down with injuries.

It is safe to assume that Wilkinson would have made the squad even if the England coach had had the luxury of a free hand in selection. He had clearly impressed Woodward when he had joined England's Five Nations squad and it was obvious to most observers that he was grooming the Newcastle starlet as a mainstay of his side for the years to come. In fact, with so many players unavailable, Wilkinson's name was probably one of the first Woodward wrote down.

The squad set off to face the southern hemisphere giants in less-than-confident mood and local Brisbane bookmakers made Australia an incredible 16–1 on to beat Woodward's inexperienced side ahead of the opening Test. England had never won a Test in Australia and no-one from either camp gave them a prayer of ending the sequence. Not even the England management could conceal the sense that the team were little more than lambs to the slaughter.

"Yes, we're scared," admitted assistant coach John Mitchell days before the game. "People expect us to be wiped out and we have to try and use that feeling to our advantage. In this part of the world you either get respect or humiliation. Humiliation, and the fear of it, is a big part of the equation."

Only five players who had started in the victory over Ireland in April were in the side that Woodward unveiled to tackle the Wallabies. Wilkinson's half-back partner, Gloucester scrum-half Scott Benton, was marginally more experienced – Wilkinson had played two minutes of international rugby, Benton three!

It was going to take a miracle for England to come away from Brisbane with an unlikely victory. In fact, the match was an unmitigated disaster as Australia ran in 11 unanswered tries in a record-breaking 76–0 victory. It was England's heaviest defeat in 127 years of international rugby and the first time they had conceded more than 50 points in a Test match. Total humiliation.

For Wilkinson, it was a miserable night; he missed two relatively easy shots at goal, and so morale-sapping was the loss that many wondered if he would ever recover from the experience.

"Who knows how the likes of Jonny Wilkinson, 19, might react to continued pummelling?" wrote Mick Cleary in the *Daily Telegraph*. "The Newcastle fly-half is an inspiring talent. One day he may be a great player. Last Saturday was not that day. As the squeeze came on, Wilkinson simply needed a few seconds of comfort, a coaxing word from a senior figure. But as he turned for that help, all he found were mirror images of himself."

And so it was on to New Zealand to face the All Blacks. If England's young guns were hoping for any respite after their humiliating mauling by the Wallabies, they were to be sorely disappointed.

The first Test in Dunedin was another massacre. The only crumbs of comfort for Wilkinson and the rest of the England team were that at least they managed to score three tries, after drawing a blank in Australia, but their eventual 64–22 defeat was still embarrassing. The tour was starting to come apart at the seams and, perhaps for the first time in his career, Wilkinson was not the star turn in a dominant team. He was just another shell-shocked member of a side, hopelessly out of its depth.

He was spared the indignity of another very public mauling when an ankle injury ruled him out of the second Test in Auckland. In retrospect, it was probably a blessing in disguise. To their credit England acquitted themselves a little better against New Zealand the second time around as they went down 40–10, but for Wilkinson the tour was over. He did not play in the final match of the trip – a 18–0 defeat against South Africa in Cape Town – and he returned to England with a lot on his mind. Here was a young man who was not used to losing and a player fiercely determined never to experience the pain of such a heavy defeat again. He vowed to return mentally stronger.

More used to being the star player in a dominant team, Wilkinson – during his first England tour to Australia – was just another member of an inexperienced side hopelessly out of its depth.

CHAPTER FIVE

THE FIGHTBACK STARTS HERE

The rest of 1998 was to prove no more positive for Wilkinson than the summer tour had been. His ankle injury eventually cleared up but the scars of his southern hemisphere nightmare would take longer to heal as England began their World Cup qualifying campaign without him. Few of the England team that went to Australia, New Zealand and South Africa were spared by Woodward when his big guns returned to the fold and Wilkinson had to content himself with club rugby.

England duly dispatched the Netherlands and Italy in their World Cup qualifiers – running up a record 110–0 scoreline against the hapless Dutch team – and were then unlucky to go down 12–11 to Australia at Twickenham in November with a side that featured just two survivors from the one blown away in Brisbane in June. A week later they beat the Springboks 13–7 at the same venue and the year came to a close. English rugby had finally restored a little pride after the tribulations of summer and the 1999 Five Nations beckoned.

For Wilkinson, 1999 was to be the year that he bounced back. England's first championship match was against Scotland at Twickenham in February and the Newcastle fly-half was recalled by Woodward to play at centre. He had been playing in midfield for the Falcons, with Rob Andrew at 10, and Woodward had no doubt that Wilkinson was ready to return to the England set-up. It was also the first time he was to be the first-choice goal-kicker in the side.

"I've been looking at all the various permutations since I knew that Phil de Glanville and Will Greenwood would be unavailable," the England coach said when he announced his team to face the Scots. "Jonny has been very strong defensively at centre. It will not be quite as pressurised for him,

although I've got no doubt he will go very well."

As soon as the media heard of his recall, Wilkinson was besieged by questions about the aftermath of the summer tour. Was he plagued by self-doubt after the experience? Did he resent being dropped by Woodward for the last four games? The teenager took it all in his stride.

"I have not watched the Australia match," he admitted. "It was a horrendous experience but, I guess, a learning experience. I was determined to come back a stronger and better player. Mind you, I did fear that it could take an awful long time to get back in the England set-up."

The Murrayfield match itself, however, was a curate's egg of a game. Although England ran out 24–21 winners, Scotland had pushed them far too close for comfort and Woodward was far from happy with the display. However, the day could hardly have gone better for Wilkinson personally. Superb in defence and sharp in attack, he landed all four of his kicks at goal. It was as if Australia and New Zealand had just been a bad dream.

"Jonny played like he had 57 caps out there today," said his centre partner Jeremy Guscott, the man who not long before had mistaken Wilkinson for an autograph-hunter. "It's great to see a 19-year-old with such composure."

Wilkinson himself was characteristically modest in his post-match summary: "I now know what international rugby is all about. It is much faster and the intensity is a great deal higher. Jerry helped me through it."

But there was no such holding back from his mentor at Newcastle, Rob Andrew. "I'm really, really pleased for Jonny and, of course, his success reflects well on Newcastle," he said. "I've had my day and enjoyed a brilliant time for which I'm very

In 1999, Wilkinson showed his true mettle, bouncing back from his nightmare Down Under to prove his international credentials.

grateful, but now the kids have a new idol. After everything he went through last summer, I prayed Jonny would land that all-important first conversion against Scotland. Being given the goal-kicking responsibilities is a hell of a position to be in at 19. But as Jonny proved, my worries were groundless.

"He's so mature it's easy to forget how young he is. I brought him to Newcastle to be groomed as my successor but don't forget he'd been playing for his school until last season and the jump from schools rugby to Five Nations over two years is absolutely unimaginable."

The apprentice was eager to return the compliment. "I've learnt so much from Rob over the last couple of seasons. He's taught me how to handle myself both on and off the pitch. Talk to any of the other coaches who worked with Rob and they'll tell you that he sweated for the things he's achieved. I can instinctively relate to that, because it's my approach too."

It was a foregone conclusion that the teenager would keep his place in the side for England's next match against Ireland in Dublin. Although he had quieter game compared to his Twickenham debut a fortnight previously, it was nonetheless a performance that hinted at his growing maturity on the international stage as Woodward's side emerged 27–15 victors. His kicking was tidy (he landed four penalties and a conversion) and the crowd had their first glimpse of his attacking potential with the ball in hand when he fired out a wide pass for Bath full-back Matt Perry to score England's first try.

The French were the visitors to Twickenham two weeks later and it was to be a fixture when England fans realised what a potent match-winner the team now had in their ranks. The team had been beaten in Paris the year before and Woodward and his men were eager for revenge. Wilkinson would deliver it. It was far from a classic encounter but few could fault Wilkinson's contribution of seven penalty kicks from seven attempts, including a monstrous 47-yard effort in the second-half, as the Tricolores were beaten 21–10.

"A lot of people will criticise me for choosing to go for the kicks," admitted England skipper Lawrence Dallaglio in the post-match press call: "But when you've got a guy like Jonny in your team, you've got to take your points."

It was, everyone agreed, a peerless performance and his 21-point haul with the boot equalled the Five Nations record of seven penalties jointly held by England's Simon Hodgkinson and, perhaps predictably, Rob Andrew.

The win over the French set England up for their first Grand Slam since 1995 and only the Welsh stood between Woodward's men and the clean sweep. Everyone predicted a comfortable English victory but, as so often happens in sport, the pundits were proved wrong.

The match was played at Wembley because Wales' new Millennium Stadium in Cardiff was still under construction in readiness for the World Cup finals later the same year. But if England thought Wales' loss of home advantage would make their task easier, they were made to think again.

Initially, the game seemed to be going to plan as England took an early lead through a Dan Luger try in only the second minute but they were unable to put themselves out of sight despite further scores from debutant winger Steve Hanley and flanker Richard Hill. Wales clung on and, with the game heading towards injury time, they found themselves trailing by just six points. The stage was set for centre Scott Gibbs to crash over for the Welsh in the dying seconds, fly-half Neil Jenkins converted to make the score 32–31 and England felt the Grand Slam wrenched from their grasp at the death.

Although they did not know it then, Wilkinson and his team-mates would have to wait much longer for their first taste of Grand Slam glory.

For Wilkinson himself, it had been far from a bad performance – he scored 16 of England 31 points – but the bitter disappointment of defeat when victory was all that mattered was only to drive him on in his pursuit of perfection.

He didn't talk to the press after the game but it was obvious that the quiet, introspective teenager in some way blamed himself for England's heartache. He went away and resolved to practice even harder.

Wilkinson scored 16 points in England's final 1999 Six Nations match against Wales, but it wasn't enough to prevent a 32–31 defeat and a Grand Slam near-miss.

CHAPTER SIX

FIRST PASS AT WORLD CUP GLORY

Luckily for Wilkinson and the rest of the England squad, there was little time for recriminations in the wake of the shock defeat to Wales. It was a World Cup year and however keenly they felt the sense of disappointment after their last-gasp surrender of the Grand Slam, a greater, global prize was up for grabs. Everyone in the England camp knew being kings of the northern hemisphere was one thing, but beating the southern hemisphere powers and lifting the World Cup was an altogether different prospect.

The fact that the tournament, although technically hosted by Wales, was to be held throughout the UK and France only added to the sense of anticipation and expectation. England may have had a dismal record against the All Blacks, Wallabies and Springboks in their own backyard, but with home advantage (Woodward's side were to enjoy the luxury of playing their group games at Twickenham) they were still a force to be reckoned with. The bookies made New Zealand the favourites, closely followed by Australia, but England had a chance.

Woodward's preparations for the competition began in earnest June that year when he assembled a squad for a one-off game against the Wallabies in Australia. It was Wilkinson's first return to the country where he had experienced his darkest moment as a player just 12 months earlier. The venue this time was Stadium Australia in Sydney – instead of Brisbane's Suncorp Stadium – but the sense that England's exciting new talent was returning to the lions' den, confidence high after an impressive Five Nations debut season, was palpable. Would he emerge unscathed this time?

England's preparations for the game were a million miles away from the ramshackle build-up to their 76–0 mauling in Brisbane and this time Woodward took a full-strength squad Down Under. The party spent four weeks training in virtual seclusion on the Queensland Gold Coast and they were confident they would show the Wallabies the real England.

It did not, however, go quite according to plan. England certainly gave Australia a run for their money but they could not quite find the extra gear they needed, going down to a creditable, but ultimately disappointing, 22–15 defeat. A little pride had been restored though and, more significantly, Wilkinson had gone some way to laying a ghost to rest with an assured and influential display. After the game, the Wallabies coach Rod Macqueen paid tribute to his performance: "He had a top night and he has a big future ahead of him."

England returned to the UK and played two more warm-up matches before the World Cup against the United States and Canada. It was Woodward's last chance to fine-tune his side and the indications were that the England engine was ticking over nicely.

Against the Americans, England ran in 16 tries in a thumping 106–8 victory at Twickenham. Although it may have been a massively, perhaps pointlessly mismatched contest, Wilkinson still went about his business with trademark diligence, converting 13 of the England scores. He had not been tested by the Americans but at least there was clearly nothing wrong with his boot.

The Canada game was a far closer encounter. England emerged 36–11 winners but new captain Martin Johnson was far from happy with the overall level of his team's performance: "It was very frustrating. It has brought us back down to earth with a bump after the America game but maybe that's what we needed."

Wilkinson was in fine kicking form in the World Cup warm-up games, but he was distraught after missing four of his eight kicks in a 30–16 defeat by New Zealand in the tournament proper.

But it was finally time for the talking to stop and the real action to begin. The fourth rugby union World Cup was about to start.

England began their campaign in early October against Italy at Twickenham, a match that propelled Wilkinson to new heights. England knew it was vital to get their challenge for the Webb Ellis trophy off to a winning, and hopefully convincing start.

They scored three tries in the first-half and five in the second in a trouble-free 67–7 victory and, significantly, Wilkinson was at the top of his game. His haul of 30 points – including his first-ever try for his country – set a new England record.

Clive Woodward could not have wished for a better opening, but sterner challenges lay ahead: the next group game was against New Zealand.

The All Blacks had denied England a place in the final four years previously after a virtuoso performance from Jonah Lomu. If Wilkinson and company were to ensure an easier passage to the 1999 final, avoiding South Africa in the quarter-finals and the Australians in the last four, they knew they had to send the Kiwis packing this time.

It was not to be. For long periods England were in contention and, with the scores tied at 16–16 in the second-half, there was a sense in the Twickenham crowd that a famous victory beckoned. They had forgotten about Lomu, who blasted his way through four English tackles for a try that irreversibly turned the tide of the match. New Zealand added another try with 10 minutes to go and England were beaten 30–16.

If it was a bad day for England, it was even worse for Wilkinson, who missed four of his eight kicks at goal. The perfectionist was inconsolable after the final whistle and although no-one was blaming him for England's defeat, he refused to take comfort from his team-mates words of encouragement in the dressing room. He admitted later that he felt his whole world had collapsed around him and he left Twickenham quickly in a dark mood.

Wilkinson didn't feature in the final group game – a 101–10 rout of Tonga – but Woodward recalled him to the side for the quarter-final play-off against Fiji. England came out 45–24 winners and despite being unceremoniously floored late on by a swinging arm from the Fiji captain Greg Smith, it was a game that went some way to helping Wilkinson put his All Blacks experience behind him.

"I was pretty pleased with my performance," he said. "It was a loose and unstructured game, and a lot of fun to play in. Much of the cynicism you encounter against other opponents was missing so the game was probably entertaining to watch. We felt the confidence to try things in the backs, some came off and a few didn't. Our only real disappointment was letting them in for a few tries."

But if the free-flowing encounter with the Fijians was to put the smile back on Wilkinson's face, it was instantly wiped off when Woodward announced his side to face South Africa in the quarter-final in Paris. To the consternation of the media and fans alike, the England coach decided to jettison Wilkinson in favour of Northampton's reliable but unspectacular Paul Grayson.

Wilkinson was inconsolable. Woodward told a packed press conference that he still envisaged the Newcastle star playing a big part from the bench in the second-half but for a player who had never accepted anything less than the best, they were hollow words. The World Cup was the stage on which he had always dreamt of playing and now the chance to display his talents in the knockout stages had been taken away. It was a bitter experience that was to further mould one of England's greatest-ever sporting talents.

Wilkinson did feature for 25 minutes of the Springboks clash but there was to be no fairy tale ending to the story for him or for England. At half-time, South Africa lead 16–12 and England were only in touch thanks to four superb penalties from Grayson. The second half was a different story. Wilkinson came on for Grayson after 55 minutes but his opposite number, Springbok fly-half Jannie de Beer, stole the headlines. De Beer had been a controversial choice in the South Africa side but he confounded his critics by landing a world record five drop goals in the second-half. England lost 44–21; Wilkinson's World Cup dream would have to wait for four, long years.

Clive Woodward controversially left Wilkinson out of the starting line-up to play South Africa in the quarter-final. He came on for 25 minutes – here seen tackling Pieter Muller – but England ended up losing 44–21.

CHAPTER SEVEN

FOLLOW THE LEADER

When Clive Woodward accepted the job as England coach, he insisted he wanted to be judged on his side's performance at the World Cup. No longer, he said, should England simply content themselves with their dominance over the Celtic sides in the Five Nations – Woodward knew the true mark of his team's progress would come on the world stage and against the very best sides.

So what had we learned about Woodward's England from the 1999 World Cup? The harsh reality was that the team had lost to New Zealand and South Africa while there was little kudos to be taken from victories over Italy, Tonga and Fiji.

But despite their untimely World Cup exit, England were heading in the right direction. Under Woodward, they were at least looking to play a more expansive game, they were finally becoming truly professional in their approach, and the gap between the team and the southern hemisphere giants was beginning to narrow.

The emergence of such a young talent as Wilkinson certainly aided Woodward's cause. He had faith in him despite Wilkinson's unprecedented lack of club experience. No previous England boss had the vision or courage to involve such an untested player at international level and, despite dropping him to the bench for the Springbok quarter-final, it seemed as though Wilkinson and Woodward's fates were intertwined.

It was now 2000 and England kicked off their campaign in the new Six Nations Championship (Italy's pleas to the member countries to be allowed to enter the tournament had finally been heard) against Ireland at Twickenham. Woodward once again turned to Wilkinson as his first-choice fly-half and records tumbled as England brushed the opposition aside. The 50–18 scoreline set a new record for the highest score in the history of a fixture that dated back to 1875 and Wilkinson landed eight of his 11 shots at goal for a personal haul of 20 points.

England had bounced back in style, but none of the players were getting carried away. The next game was in Paris, the scene of their South African mugging, and they all knew that the French capital had not been the happiest of hunting grounds over the years. "Today was just a start," said Mike Catt after the Ireland win. "Paris is something of a bogey venue for us. Time to put the record straight."

That is exactly what England did but they were hugely indebted to both Wilkinson's boot and his phenomenal power in the tackle. England won a scrappy, ugly game 15–9, Wilkinson scoring all the points with five penalties, but it was one tackle he made on French winger Emile Ntamack in the first-half that was to be the turning point of the match. 9–0 down, the French were pushing hard in the dying minutes of the half and worked Ntamack free, with only Wilkinson to beat. The smart money was on the powerful Frenchman but Wilkinson thumped him backwards with such force that the crowd gasped. England went in at the break without conceding any points and France were never able to get within striking distance again.

"It was one of the best tackles I've ever seen," an upbeat Woodward said after the match. "I was the first into the changing room at half-time and you should have seen the guys in there. They were so pumped up."

England's coach was also quick to highlight the growing maturity in his fly-half's game: "The major difference now is that he's surrounded by even younger players and his leadership skills are coming through on the pitch, where he is 'the man'.

By 2000, Clive Woodward was hailing Wilkinson's maturity, but the man himself argued that he was still far from the finished article.

I made the call to leave him out against South Africa in the World Cup. I thought it was best for him. He's a tough character and he came through it."

Wilkinson himself was reluctant to accept talk of him being the finished article after just 16 caps. "I'd never say I'm a senior player now but I suppose I'm a little bit more relaxed and more willing to add my own input. People spoke of Rob Andrew as the complete fly-half only after he'd played for many years. Michael Lynagh was the same. I'm in a different park to them. Fly-halves only ever seem to pick up titles at the end of their careers."

For once, Wilkinson would be proved wrong.

England's next match took them back to the comfort of Twickenham and the visit of the Welsh. If England were still smarting from having the Grand Slam snatched from them at Wembley the previous season, they didn't show it. England's forwards took the game by the scruff of the neck and suffocated the life out of Wales. The home team were comfortable 46–12 winners and Wilkinson racked up another 21 points. England were two games away from the elusive Grand Slam.

A historic first championship clash with Italy in Rome's Stadio Flaminio followed and although it was not his most scintillating performance for his country, Wilkinson captured yet another record. England comfortably beat the Azzurri 59–12 and, despite being substituted seven minutes from time with the game won, Wilkinson's tally of 12 points from two penalties and three conversions took his total for the championship season to 70, eclipsing the previous best by 1980s full-back Jonathan Webb. Although the record books will show Wilkinson broke the record in the first season of the newly-formed Six, rather than Five Nations, he actually overtook Webb's mark in exactly the same number of games. A man who had still not turned 21 was continuing to rewrite rugby history.

All that now stood between England and the Grand Slam was Scotland at Murrayfield. Wilkinson and company were overwhelming favourites and there were few Scottish fans who genuinely believed that their side were capable of upsetting the odds. Surely Woodward and his team would not be denied the clean sweep for a second successive season?

But the match turned into a nightmare and it was Scotland's Number 10 Duncan Hodge, and not the English fly-half, who was to enjoy the plaudits at the final whistle. In driving wind and sleet, England looked uncharacteristically nervous while the Scots produced a fiery performance to emerge 19–13 winners. An inspired Hodge scored all of his side's points, including the match's decisive try six minutes from the end.

The questions about England's mental strength at the crunch remained unanswered and for Wilkinson and the rest of the squad, there was a real sense of failure. They had played some thrilling rugby in the championship, yet they had fallen again at the final hurdle and the Grand Slam seemed as elusive as ever.

The year, however, was to have a happy ending for the England team. A two-Test series in South Africa in June beckoned, followed by the visit of Australia, Argentina and a return fixture with the Springboks at Twickenham. The side would once again quickly shake off their disappointment and, in doing so, put down a real marker for the next World Cup, which was now just two years away.

The squad set off for South Africa in good heart. The Springboks, the experts argued, were there for the taking. As ever though, much would depend on Wilkinson. Sadly, England's best laid plans were torn to shreds on the morning of the first Test in Pretoria when the Newcastle fly-half had to pull out. He had been up all the previous night suffering from vomiting and diarrhoea. Leicester utility man Austin Healey was drafted in as emergency cover at fly-half and England started the game in unfamiliar shape.

Wilkinson's late withdrawal proved decisive. Although England produced a performance full of grit and power, they sorely missed his controlling influence and despite scoring the only try of the match, they lost 18–13. It was a reminder just how indispensable he had become to the side.

It was doubtful whether Wilkinson would recover in time for the second Test in Bloemfontein the following week and some England followers began

Left: Wilkinson helped England end 2000 on a high, scoring 20 of England's points in a 25–17 win over South Africa. Overleaf: Scotland's Gregor Townsend gets to grips with England's number 10.

to suspect that their idol had been the victim of a Springbok plot. Five years earlier, New Zealand claimed their squad were the victims of deliberate food poisoning on the eve of their World Cup final with hosts South Africa (the Springboks won the final against all expectations) and now the whispers began that Wilkinson had also been nobbled.

The man himself was having none of it. "There was no foul play involved here," he said two days before the second Test. "My appetite hadn't been good but I put that down to the effects of altitude. I felt a bit queasy going to bed on the Friday night but nothing untoward. I felt in the morning that I might be able to play but the management thought differently. It was the right decision."

There was a collective sigh of relief when Wilkinson was cleared to play in Bloemfontein and England set their sights on squaring the series. And so it was as England clinched a bruising encounter 27–22 with Wilkinson the undisputed hero of the hour. The fly-half scored all of his side's points with eight penalties and a drop goal – he alone was the difference between victory and defeat. England had only their second win in their last 15 attempts against the southern hemisphere and it was only their fifth win in their history south of the Equator.

For Wilkinson, who spent three days in bed in the build-up to the match with what turned out to be a gastric bug, it was a huge effort: "I was dying a death out there in the first 20 minutes. Lining up the penalties actually gave me a breather!"

Clive Woodward, usually so cautious in his exchanges with the media, could hardly contain himself. "Jonny is now the player I wanted him to be. He's really come out of himself. It took Rob Andrew a while to find himself as a Test stand-off. It's the same with Jonny. He is undoubtedly the man now, the voice that commands."

No doubt Wilkinson would have blushed if he'd heard his coach's gushing tribute but no-one could argue with Woodward's sentiments. At the age of 21, and with 20 caps under his belt, he was now a fully-fledged international player.

England headed for home and a well-earned break before the autumn internationals with Australia, Argentina and the South Africans.

Reigning World Cup champions Australia were certainly wary, maybe even a tad fearful, of the threat Wilkinson posed to their own relatively inexperienced team in the aftermath of his virtuoso performance against South Africa.

"He is a very big ingredient in the England mix," Australia coach Rod Macqueen said pre-match. "He makes their backline unpredictable. He takes gaps when they're there and has a great pass that can put players away. He keeps the opposition on their toes and that makes for an intelligent side. England missed his organisational skills when he didn't play in the World Cup."

Macqueen was right to be wary. England, clinically prompted and prodded by Wilkinson, were superb against the Australians and after a dramatic injury-time try in the second-half from winger Dan Luger, they emerged 22–19 victors.

England had beaten the Australians for the first time in five years – it was also Wilkinson's first triumph against the men from Down Under in three attempts – and it was the first time they had recorded back-to-back wins against southern hemisphere opposition since 1994. Everything in the England garden was rosy.

Next up was Argentina and although there was little to shout about in England's stuttering, error-strewn performance, they did at least win the game 19–0. Wilkinson, like his team-mates, was not at his best but he still kicked 14 points from three penalties, a conversion and a drop goal. Significantly, his haul took him past the 300-point barrier in international rugby and he became the youngest player ever to pass that milestone.

The year ended for England against the Springboks. After the heartache of their Grand Slam failure, it was important that it was to finish on a winning note. Once again, Wilkinson was the opposition's chief tormentor, clocking up 20 points with the boot as well as conjuring up a deft, one-handed pass for centre Will Greenwood to score the home side's only try in a 25–17 win.

England were clearly a side going places and Wilkinson was their undisputed star turn.

Phil Vickery gives England's main man a well-earned hug.

CHAPTER EIGHT

"THE BEST NUMBER 10 IN THE WORLD"

For Wilkinson and his England colleagues, 2001 was to be a massive year. The Six Nations lay ahead of them and there was another chance to win the Grand Slam which their performances over the previous two years had deserved. There was also the prospect of the British Lions tour to Australia that summer to consider and Wilkinson was determined that he was not going to miss out.

His performances for England in 2000 should have made him an automatic choice in Graham Henry's touring party but there were no guarantees that Wales' New Zealander coach would see things that way. Wilkinson would have to prove himself all over again to ensure he was on the plane Down Under and the Six Nations would provide him with the perfect platform on which to state his case.

England kicked off their campaign against Henry's Wales in Cardiff, thus giving Wilkinson ample opportunity to show the Lions coach what he was all about. It would also give the England fly-half a chance to silence the critics who argued that Wales' Neil Jenkins, rather than Wilkinson, should be the Lions' first choice Number 10.

Wilkinson won both battles hands down as England stormed to a record-breaking 44–15 victory – it was England's highest score and biggest winning margin in Cardiff. Wilkinson easily over-shadowed his opposite number: England's Number 10 landed five of his seven attempts at goal in an assured all-round display while Jenkins struggled throughout and was on target with just two of his five shots at the posts.

"That was as good a display as I've seen from a European side in a long time," conceded Henry afterwards. "England were far too good for us."

Former England fly-half Stuart Barnes went much further, writing: "In recent weeks, there has been a growing band pushing Jenkins as the likely Test outside-half for the Lions in Australia. These errant souls now know better. Jenkins is like a wonderful musician in an orchestra. He can play his instrument beautifully, whatever tune he is told to play, though one or two notes do not come easily. In contrast, Wilkinson does not so much play as conduct."

Italy were England's next opponents, and after 27 uninspiring minutes the unfancied visitors to Twickenham were surprise 20–17 leaders. England battled to a 10-point lead at the break but emerged in the second-half unrecognisable from the lacklustre XV that had huffed and puffed in the first 40 minutes, running in seven tries (including one from Wilkinson) to post an emphatic 80–23 victory. England were just getting better and better and their stand-off was revelling in the team's success.

For the all-conquering Number 10, it was another personal triumph. His 35-point tally set a new individual Six Nations record and he also passed both his mentor Rob Andrew and Paul Grayson as England's highest-ever points scorer in the competition with 187. The fact that he missed the 14th and final kick at goal (which would have moved him ahead of Grayson in the all-time England's scoring charts) mattered little. Wilkinson was now surely the first name on Graham Henry's list of players to tackle the Wallabies.

"I think that Jonny is the world's best Number 10," Woodward enthused. "He had a fantastic game and I can't think of anything he cannot do."

Wilkinson too was upbeat, albeit briefly, in his post-match interviews. "It is great when people like Clive say nice things like that," he said before introducing his now customary bout of self-doubt. "But I have got my weaknesses and I just want to keep getting better and better."

Right: Getting off on the right foot – kicking off against Scotland in the Six Nations. Overleaf: Another successful kick in England's record-breaking victory over Wales.

NIVEA for MEN
EXIT
EXIT
Computacenter
TETLEY'S
TETLEY'S
Lloyds TSB
Lloyds TSB
Lloyds TSB
Lloyds TSB

If the England Number 10 had produced a near-faultless display against Italy at Twickenham, his radar was inexplicably to desert him just seven days later when he returned to the home of English rugby with his club Newcastle.

The Falcons had reached the final of the Tetley's Bitter Cup and, for once, Wilkinson's exploits at club level rather than his performances for England were to take centre stage. The fly-half had been a perhiperal figure in the club's 1998 League triumph – it was his first season in the north east – and this was the opportunity for him to repay Rob Andrew and company for their part in his meteroic rise. Sadly, Wilkinson will not look back on the game with great fondness, despite leaving Twickenham with a winner's medal around his neck.

Newcastle's opponents were Harlequins and the London side lead the match from the 15th minute to the last, but Falcons full-back Dave Walder scored in the fourth minute of injury time to snatch a dramatic, if unlikely victory. Wilkinson converted to complete a 30–27 win but it had not been a good day at the office. He had been as abrasive as ever in defence, but his kicking was wayward and he landed just four of his eight goal attempts. In contrast, his opposite number Paul Burke returned a cup final record of 22 points despite being on the losing side.

Typically though, Wilkinson was eager not to take the gloss off his team-mates triumph at the final whistle, saying, "It was brilliant for us to win silverware at club level. It is important as a player to be part of a club which can offer you the chance to develop and where you have a good shot at winning leagues and cups. At Newcastle there is that potential and this final was a great start."

But the Number 10 knew he had not performed to his own exacting standards and he consoled himself with the knowledge there was still a Six Nations job to do for England.

Scotland's visit to Twickenham in the third match of the tournament for England was only marginally less painful than it had been for Italy two weeks before and a clinical display saw Woodward's team run out 43–3 winners. Now, only France and Ireland could stop them finally fulfilling their destiny and completing the Grand Slam.

Sadly, England's next game with the French was robbed of some of its potential drama before kick-off. If England won, they knew they would have to beat Ireland in Dublin to complete the clean sweep, but the foot-and-mouth epidemic caused the Irish RFU to announce the rest of the Six Nations fixtures, including the England game, would be played in the autumn, after the Lions tour. Even if France were dispatched, Woodward's men would have to wait six months before the crunch match. If England were disappointed, they did not show it and the match was to prove a symbolic one for Wilkinson and his Newcastle mentor, Rob Andrew.

At first, things did not go England's way, Wilkinson uncharacteristically missing his opening pop at goal, as France's powerful forwards took control. At half-time, trailing 16–13, the men in white knew they had a fight on their hands. But they rose to the challenge superbly, pulling away from the fading French to win convincingly 48–19.

For Wilkinson, it was another moment of destiny. His 18 points took his tally for his country to 407 in Tests and he had finally overtaken the previous best mark of 396 set by Andrew himself. The apprentice had eclipsed the master.

Newcastle's director of rugby had said back in 1998 that he fully expected his young charge to beat his England record. But it is doubtful if even he could have envisaged how quickly Wilkinson would smash it – reaching the milestones after 27 caps when it had taken Andrew 70 games to reach his tally. There were now few records left to break.

With the Six Nations on unavoidable hold, thoughts turned once again to the Lions tour to Australia. Predictably, Henry unveiled an English-dominated squad for the challenge ahead and Wilkinson was named alongside Jenkins and Ireland's Ronan O'Gara at Number 10 for the trip. The England star was to return again to the scene of his worst international experience, but this time he was older and wiser and he would be playing alongside the cream of British and Irish rugby. Could he and the Lions return home victorious?

Wilkinson wasn't on top form in Newcastle's Tetley's Bitter Cup final win over Harlequins, but the Falcons still edged the London side 30–27.

CHAPTER NINE

DESPAIR OF A WOUNDED LION

The Lions set off for Australia from Heathrow airport on Friday 1 June 2001, in the knowledge that within the next six hectic weeks they had a golden chance to cement their own place in rugby folklore by beating the World Cup-winning Wallabies. Six days of intense preparation and team-building at a secluded Hampshire training camp had achieved it's aim of bonding the 50-strong party together and they boarded the plane in buoyant and confident mood.

At just 22, Lions rookie Wilkinson was one of the younger members of the 37-man playing squad, but he had no reason at all to feel overawed. His performances for England during the preceding two-and-a-half years had earned him the respect of his new Irish, Welsh and Scottish team-mates and it also helped that he sat on the plane alongside 17 of his England colleagues, who made up the bulk of Graham Henry's Lions squad. The importance of the moment wasn't lost on him. "Being selected for the Lions is different to being picked for England," he admitted. "Not better or worse, just very different because living with the Lions is all about here and now. The opportunity to play with these guys from the other Home Nations for whom I have so much admiration, isn't something that I want to waste."

After an energy-sapping 22-hour journey via Singapore, the exhausted Lions landed in Perth to begin preparations for the first Test in Brisbane four weeks later. Wilkinson wasn't totally relaxed though, as he hadn't arrived in Australia in the greatest physical condition. The demands of a long domestic season had taken their toll and a nagging groin injury was causing him problems.

As a result, the usual full-blooded training regime and painstaking kicking practice to which he'd become accustomed had to be put on hold as the Lions medical staff nursed him back into shape for the battles ahead. It meant that both Ireland's Ronan O'Gara and Wales' Neil Jenkins had a chance to stake their own claims for a place at Number 10 in the Test side in the first two games.

The opening fixture turned out to be an embarrassingly one-sided affair on a rainy evening at the WACA, with the Lions trouncing Western Australia by a record score of 116–10, breaking the previous record of 97 points by the Lions which had stood since 1974. Wilkinson was also a spectator in sultry Townsville, where the Lions easily dispatched a Queensland Presidents XV 83–6, scoring a mammoth 73 unanswered points in a superb second-half display.

The team appeared to be taking shape nicely, but agonisingly for Wilkinson he'd yet to make any mark at all. That was soon to change.

With his groin fully recovered, the Newcastle fly-half finally made his Lions debut on Saturday 16 June against a strong Queensland Reds side, packed full of experienced Wallabies' internationals. The Reds provided the Lions with their stiffest test to date, but Wilkinson wasn't fazed one bit, turning in a man-of-the-match display. His inch-perfect kick created the first try for Dan Luger, an incisive pass put Richard Hill over for the fourth Lions try just before half-time, and it was also Wilkinson's clever break which paved the way for Brian O'Driscoll's second-half score. In between, the young pretender had also landed seven out of eight kicks. The boy wonder had made his mark.

"Wilkinson conducted the match with all the aplomb of a master musician," gushed Alistair Hignell in the *Daily Telegraph*. "The young playmaker had been kept back for this match and

Practising his kicking like a man possessed in Brisbane.

responded with a virtuoso display that did everything to justify Clive Woodward's boast that he is already the best Number 10 in the world."

Wilkinson's performance against the Reds had undoubtedly confirmed him as a Test certainty in Graham Henry's mind and his omission from the next tour game against Australia A signalled to one and all that the coach was wrapping his star man in cotton wool for the three-game Test series.

The next build-up game against the NSW Waratahs was dominated by predictions of an all-out war, and those prophecies turned out to be true. A violent match was won by the likely Lions Test XV 41–24, but it was a below-par display from the tourists. Wilkinson had a solid but unspectacular game, kicking two penalties and all four of his conversions, as well as going over for his first-ever Lions try in the second-half. But, in truth, it was hard for anyone to shine in a game marred by ill-discipline.

Despite playing just 154 minutes on tour, Wilkinson was a cast-iron certainty to play in the first Test and even the one-eyed Australian press had now realised that his upcoming duel with Stephen Larkham was a genuine battle between the two best fly-halves in the world. But all was not well in the Lions camp. Lawrence Dallaglio, Mike Catt and Neil Back were all injured and there were rumblings of discontent in the dressing room.

"I went to see Jonny at the team hotel with a couple of friends two days before the first Test and I could tell that the nerves were really jangling," said his father Phil, who had flown out to watch. "Jonny is always calm on the outside and he still was, but I could sense that he and the rest of the boys were all a little tense."

For Wilkinson though, this game wasn't just about the Lions. He was in Brisbane, and the last time he'd been to the capital of Queensland three years before, he'd been humiliated in that record-breaking 76–0 loss to the Wallabies. "That loss has been one of the biggest factors in my career since," he said. "It was a heavy hit to take at that time but, if you told me that I needed to take it to be here now, then I would take it every time. It wasn't a

great feeling, but it has been very important to me in the subsequent events in my career."

Inside the Lions dressing room, the legendary ex-skipper Willie John McBride issued an emotion-charged rallying speech as the shirts were handed out to the players and all of a sudden the tide seemed to be turning. The negativity which had plagued the build-up all week had been replaced by a surge of positive thinking. Jonny Wilkinson and the rest of the Lions were ready to be unleashed from their cage.

The two sides entered the arena in front of 37,000 fans and the stadium was awash with red. Everywhere the team looked they saw friendly supportive faces. After four years of waiting, Lions fever was back.

"The one thing that I will never forget about that first Test was the scene which greeted us that night as we made our way onto the pitch," Wilkinson later said. "To see more than half of the crowd – there must have been 20,000 – in red shirts was incredible. We ran out there in disbelief and the players all looked towards each other thinking, 'What the hell is going on'. It was amazing."

Pre-match predictions suggested that the Lions would narrowly win by pounding away up front and relying on the trusty boot of Wilkinson. But, as it turned out, Wilkinson was just one excellent part of an all-round fantastic team performance. There was no need to rely on penalties as the Lions obliterated the world champions with a free-flowing, commanding display.

Wilkinson was involved in the move which led to Jason Robinson's astonishing second-minute try and was always at the heart of the Lions' best attacks but, unusually for him, his kicking wasn't as accurate as normal. He missed kicks, and not even his three successful conversions and a penalty could make up for that crime in his own mind as the Lions cantered to a 29–13 win.

Back in the dressing room the fly-half was shattered. He'd played a huge part in one of the greatest Lions victories ever, but couldn't really savour the moment knowing that he had missed three times. The team's success had given him

Taken off the pitch with what appeared to be a serious leg injury, against Australia.

satisfaction, but he quietly left the stadium a disappointed man. It wasn't the Test debut for the Lions he'd dreamed of.

But, aware that few would understand his own personal frustrations, Wilkinson diplomatically remained upbeat in his post-match interviews. "Beating the world champions Australia in their own backyard is special, and to do it so convincingly by that scoreline is incredible," he said. "And, psychologically, going 1–0 up in the series has also given us a massive boost."

The lack of celebrations at the final whistle, not just from Wilkinson but from the rest of the team too, also told a story. The job wasn't finished and they knew it.

The rest of the week saw Wilkinson practice his kicking like a man possessed. The Australian press had been mildly critical of him after Brisbane, sensing that he wasn't quite as infallible as his reputation suggested. What they wrote didn't bother Wilkinson in the slightest, but he wasn't used to missing kicks and he had to put it right. The second Test couldn't come quickly enough.

And at half-time in the Colonial Stadium, the Lions were riding the crest of a wave. Leading 11–6, the series was well and truly in their sights before a nightmare final 40 minutes, one of the worst in Lions' history, saw their dreams shattered.

Although his kicking was back to it's best, a moment of madness from Wilkinson early in the second-half just outside his own 22 when he tried to release Rob Henderson on the right wing with an ambitious looped pass cost the Lions dear. Fatally, the pass didn't have enough height and Wallaby winger Joe Roff intercepted, gathered the ball and ran in for a classic breakaway try.

Lions coach Graham Henry described the moment as "crucial" after the game, as it gave the Aussies the lift they needed to get back to 11–11, and for the rest of the game they ran amok, eventually beating the Lions by a record 35–14 score.

"Some people put the entire Lions Test series loss on my shoulders for that one pass," Wilkinson later said. "But to be honest, if that situation arose again, I'd still make the same pass. The only

difference would be that I'd make it a higher pass. I don't think I can remember hardly any other passes in my career that have been intercepted for tries, so what a time for it to happen!

"I wasn't as hard on myself for that pass as I normally am when I miss kicks. With open play it's different. After all, the try only made it 11–11 and there was a long way to go in the match. I said, 'Sorry guys, let's start again at 0–0' and that was it. My disappointment didn't last too long."

If that wayward pass wasn't bad enough, things got much, much worse for the fly-half. Five minutes from time, as he flew into a tackle on Wallabies winger Daniel Herbert, Wilkinson stayed down on the turf in agony with what appeared to be a serious leg injury. After being carried off the field on a stretcher holding his head in his hands, nobody expected Wilkinson to have any chance of being fit for the third and final Test just seven days later. In a state of panic, dad Phil frantically made his way to the dressing room,

"I'd never seen anything like it," he recalls. "It was like a scene from a battlefield with big men in agony, crying, and with five or six of them being stitched up for one thing or another. Jonny looked in a very bad way and already had his left leg elevated and packed in ice. He was then quickly whisked off to hospital."

Tour manager Donal Lenihan told RTE after the game, "Jonny has gone for checks on his lower left leg. We don't know if it's bruising or a break yet."

Thankfully tests showed that Wilkinson hadn't fractured his fibula, but the doctors at the hospital still put his left leg in plaster as a precaution. The Lions management were facing up to the fact that their star Number 10 was unlikely to be available for the crucial tour decider.

While the rest of the squad flew off to Sydney in the morning, Wilkinson stayed behind in Melbourne with team doctor James Robson for further medical checks. When morning came, after a series of scan results showed no fracture, Jonny decided he had no time to waste. He wanted the plaster cast removed, he believed he could make it.

As he limped out of the team hotel bound for the

Left: Chatting over his 'Lazarus'-style recovery from injury with kicking coach Dave Aldred during training at Keirle Park;
Overleaf: A tense moment in the Third Test.

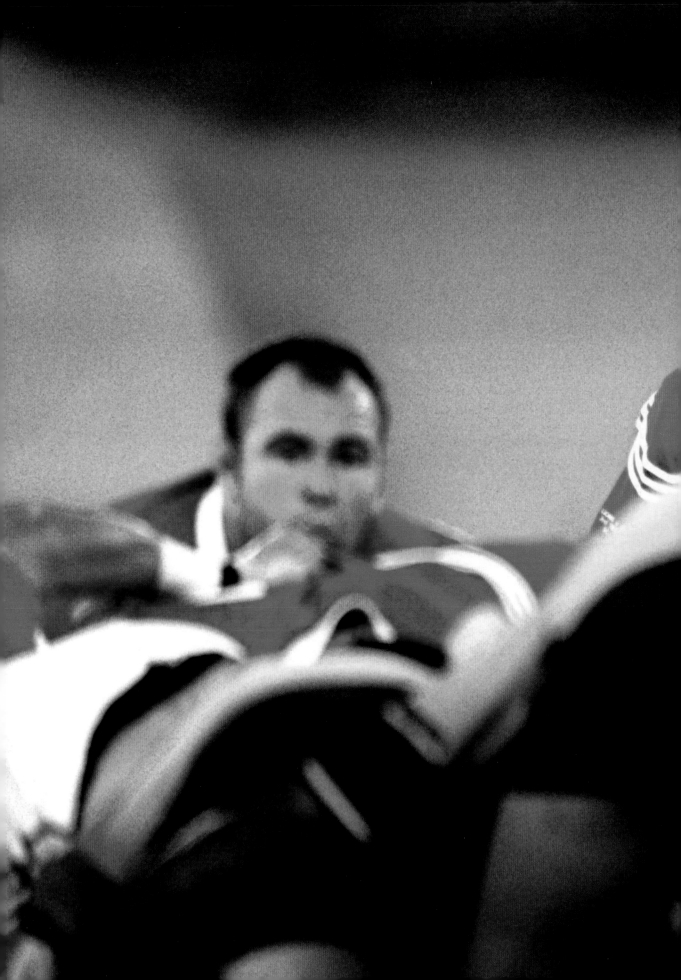

airport without the cast or crutches, Wilkinson was quizzed by reporters as to the extent of his injury. He responded in typically non-committal style. "I'm playing it by ear. It's bearing up."

The next two days were critical and he became obsessed with reducing the swelling. Under the supervision of Robson, Wilkinson underwent four swimming pool sessions, three gym work-outs, and several physiotherapy and massage sessions each day. To have any chance of being selected, the fluid on his lower left leg just had to be gone.

Wednesday was D-day for Wilkinson. He had to take part in the training session to be considered for selection. Most of the swelling had gone but the medics still warned him to take the session very lightly. Unsurprisingly, in the pouring Sydney rain, he ignored their advice as he pushed himself to the absolute limits in a bid to catch Henry's eye. He was in pain, but it worked. Later that day he was named as Number 10 for the final Test.

Scrum-half Matt Dawson still recalls that Wednesday's training session with amusement: "The lads gave him plenty of stick for the Lazarus-style recovery. For him to go down with a suspected broken leg on the Saturday, and to then be back playing a few days later was just embarrassing! We ribbed him for making more of his original injury, but we were definitely glad to see him fit."

The third and final Test match in front of 84,000 fans at Stadium Australia proved to be a fitting finale to a wonderfully entertaining series, but ultimately for the Lions it ended in failure.

The match was close with the Lions looking the most likely winners throughout. But a series of missed opportunities and ill-discipline among the forwards proved to be the difference, as full-back Matt Burke converted two late penalties to seal a narrow 29–23 Wallabies win. For Wilkinson it was yet another night of mixed emotions. Playing through the pain barrier, he scored a wonderful individual try – his first in a Test for the Lions – but when the pressure kicks came his way late in the match, his usually reliable left boot deserted him. Three relatively straightforward penalties by his standards went begging and it cost the Lions dear.

Former England international Stuart Barnes claimed the series defeat was almost entirely down to Wilkinson's 'ace card' letting him down when he needed it most. "Had the 'old' Jonny Wilkinson been kicking to his usual Twickenham standards, the Lions might just have won the series," he said. "When Wilkinson had the chance to hurt Australia, he failed too often. A 54 per cent strike rate going into the decider required dramatic improvement. Five kicks from eight was not what was required, and the three he missed were all eminently kickable by his standards."

At the final whistle, Newcastle's brilliant fly-half cut a forlorn figure. Considering the state of his left leg just seven days before, it was an amazing achievement for him to be on the pitch at all, but that cut no ice with him. The perfectionist that he is would not allow him to think like that. Six weeks of hard graft, nerves and raw emotion had culminated in the empty feeling of defeat. The chance to be part of Lions folklore had for now passed him by and his dream of lifting the 2003 World Cup in the very same stadium now seemed a million miles away.

But despite the overwhelming sense of under-achievement felt by Wilkinson, he still had every reason to feel proud of what he'd done for the Lions. He was top points scorer on tour with 72, he'd broken the record for points scored by a Lion against Australia with 36, and his 18 in the first Test had equalled the record held by Gavin Hastings for the most scored in a single Test.

"They were a defining three games in Jonny's career," his father Phil said later. "He matured greatly after the emotions he went through and, looking back, I still think it was a great tour for him."

It would take time, however, before the son would share his father's sentiments. As he wearily trudged around Stadium Australia on the Lions' "lap of honour" thanking the hordes of fans in red shirts who'd added such colour to the whole tour, he was already thinking ahead. England had a delayed date with Ireland for a Grand Slam decider and the World Cup was getting closer and closer.

Back in action, if not quite kicking to his normal high standard, in the decisive Third Test against Australia.

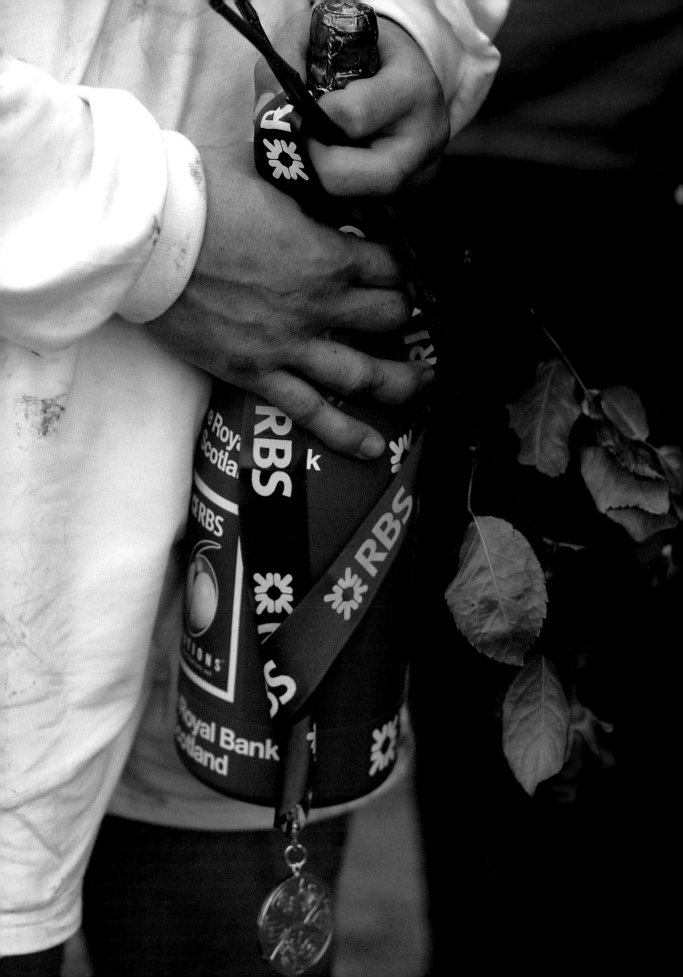

CHAPTER TEN

HOW THE GRAND SLAM WAS FINALLY WON

With his bloodied mouth stitched up, and his left shoulder throbbing with pain, Jonny Wilkinson is not for the first time in his life the centre of attention. The world's cameras are focused on his exhausted frame as he utters the words he'd been waiting his whole life to say: "It feels great to be a Grand Slam winner at last and I plan to enjoy every minute of it."

The date is Sunday 30 March 2003. The venue Lansdowne Road. England's star fly-half has just inspired Clive Woodward's side to their first Six Nations Grand Slam triumph with a sensational individual display in a 42–6 thumping of Ireland in Dublin. The weight of being labelled a "bottler" after England's previous Grand Slam failures has been lifted from his shoulders in an instant. He smiles at everyone, dropping his usual ultra-controlled persona in a rare show of public emotion, signing autographs for dozens of star-struck kids on his way back to the jubilant England dressing room. Wilkinson is a happy young man.

But first back to October 2001. After sweeping all before them in their opening four Six Nations games earlier in the year, England had had to wait until the autumn, and the end of the Lions tour, before finishing the job. The foot-and-mouth crisis had forced the fixture against the Irish to be postponed, but Woodward's team, who were on an 11-match winning streak, were still red-hot favourites to win when the game was finally replayed,

The script, however, went badly awry. An Irish side inspired by captain Keith Wood rolled over the English invaders 20–14 with a powerful and determined display that had Woodward reaching for his drawing board. Three cooly-struck penalties from Wilkinson had kept England in the game, but he and the rest of his team-mates knew they'd blown yet another golden opportunity to win that elusive Grand Slam. At the final whistle Wilkinson picked up yet another Six Nations winner's championship medal, but as he and the rest of the crestfallen England squad watched the victorious Ireland side milk their "lap of honour", they hardly felt like winners.

It was time for the young fly-half to dust himself down and start again. England now had the autumn Tests against Australia, Romania and South Africa to contend with and, like it or not, there was little time for a Dublin post-mortem.

The healing process began three weeks later when England defeated world champions Australia 21–15 in front of a cock-a-hoop Twickenham crowd. The afternoon belonged to Wilkinson as he kicked all 21 of England's points with two drop goals and five out of six penalty kicks. His personal points haul made him England's all-time leading scorer against the Aussies… at the age of just 22.

But after the match, a stunned Wilkinson found himself having to defend his team for failing to score a try, rather than talk about the fact that they'd just beaten the world champions. He told the BBC: "They defended so well that we decided to see if we could get three points when they were on offer. Against Australia you've got to keep the scoreboard ticking over."

Woodward rested his star man for the friendly against Romania a week later and, as a result, Wilkinson missed out on two more records. The 44 points scored by his replacement Charlie Hodgson broke the England record for most points scored in one game, and the team's 134–0 win was also a world-record winning margin.

Refreshed, Wilkinson prepared himself tirelessly for the Test against South Africa the following

Austin Healey hugs England's all-time leading scorer against the Aussies!

weekend, and it paid off handsomely as he converted seven penalties in a brutal 29–9 victory over the Springboks. He, and his team-mates were back on song. Surely 2002 was going to the year to break the Grand Slam hoodoo?

Before the turn of the year, Rob Andrew, Newcastle's Director of Rugby, rewarded his star fly-half with a lucrative new contract. Considering the nurturing and trusting relationship the two men had built up, there was little anxiety that he would not put pen to paper but it was still a relief that the 22-year-old was only too happy to extend his stay at Kingston Park.

"Jonny is an integral part of this club and I want him to stay here for his whole career," Andrew told the media after the ink was dry on the deal. "I want him to be to Newcastle what Martin Johnson is to Leicester. Jonny is growing in maturity and I see him as a future captain of this club." Andrew, it would be proved, was spot on in that respect.

It was not long, however, before England duties were once again on the agenda and the quest for that elusive clean sweep began at Murrayfield in February 2002, as the side looked to avenge the mauling they received on their previous visit to Edinburgh two years before. Wilkinson later admitted he was more nervous than usual ahead of the match after months spent stewing on the Ireland defeat in Dublin. In fact, Wilkinson was more wound up than he could ever remember.

As it turned out, the Calcutta Cup clash was a low-key affair as England cruised to a comfortable, if unspectacular, 29–3 win. The only concern was a knock to Wilkinson a minute from time which forced him to leave the field. But, in truth, it was a regular day at the office for all those in white shirts.

Ireland were visitors to Twickenham a fortnight later when Wilkinson – and England – exacted perfect revenge for their October defeat in Dublin. Woodward's troops demolished the men in green with a crushing display of power and guile, winning 45–11, with Wilkinson chipping in with a superb 20-point haul of his own, including his third international try, scorching over the line after good work from Ben Kay and Steve Thompson.

"Relief and joy" summed up the feelings in the dressing room after the game said Wilkinson, and you could understand why.

Confidence couldn't have been much higher as England flew out to Paris for the crucial fixture against France. Their excellent form in the autumn internationals had moved them to the top of the world rankings for the first time and they officially arrived at the Stade de France as the best team on the planet. Perhaps the rain clouds which loitered over the French capital on the morning of the game were a sign that all was not going to go to plan for Woodward's men though. Heavy rain before kick-off made conditions in the Stade de France treacherous, and that was only going to be to France's advantage. And so it proved, as at half-time trailing 17–0, England's Grand Slam dreams were in grave danger of being washed away.

Wilkinson just couldn't stamp his authority on the game, despite a couple of raking touchline kicks, and he was substituted by Woodward late on in the second-half. The move, however, wasn't enough to save England as they went down to a shock 20–15 defeat. On the day they weren't good enough and they knew it.

The French defeat hurt Wilkinson badly and he spent the next fortnight reassessing his own game. He just wasn't prepared to be nullified in the same way against the Welsh. He had to prove himself to the world all over again.

Thankfully, the sun was shining at Twickenham on a glorious late March afternoon, but Wilkinson's performance shone even brighter. His 30 points made him the first Englishman to pass the 500-point barrier in Tests and also the record English points scorer against Wales. His second-half try, when he shimmied his way past the Welsh line, was a beauty. In a game of mediocrity, Wilkinson was simply outstanding.

But as England lined up for their final Six Nations game against Italy, they already knew that France had won the competition. There was little to play for but pride, and it showed as England ran out easy, but uninspired 45–9 victors in Rome. Wilkinson's five conversions and one penalty were

Signed, sealed, and continuing to deliver for the Newcastle Falcons.

a decent return, but this was a campaign that would soon be forgotten.

After taking the summer off to recharge his batteries, Wilkinson was refreshed and back in action for his country in the autumn of 2002 when England took on the ultimate challenge of the southern hemisphere in three back-to-back home Tests playing against the All Blacks, Wallabies and Springboks. Ahead of the 2003 World Cup this was a huge test for Woodward's men, and it was time for them, and especially Wilkinson, to seize the moment.

It all began with the visit of New Zealand. At a cold but dry Twickenham, the pre-match atmosphere was electric among the capacity crowd who sang their hearts out with a roaring rendition of "Swing Low Sweet Chariot" in an attempt to drown out the All Blacks' pre-match haka. It worked too, as England blitzed the under-strength visitors with a pulsating first-half display.

Following the script to the letter, Wilkinson made his own indelible mark on the game with a brilliant individual try just after the break. Shaping up for a drop goal, the Newcastle man chipped over the static New Zealand defence, before collecting the bouncing ball under the posts. It appeared to be a moment of genius, but Wilkinson later admitted that it wasn't quite as clever as it looked:

"My chip was meant for Jason Robinson, not me! It was only after I started my run that I realised I was in the best position to go for it."

The nerve wracking 31–28 victory was only England's fifth ever win over New Zealand and Wilkinson's try, drop goal, two conversions and three penalties had been the key to their success. It was another man-of-the-match display and his reputation as the world's best fly-half was now cemented.

After the game, however, Wilkinson once again found himself defending England's tactics. "Yes, we would like to have spread the ball more," he admitted. "Yes, we would like to have broken the gain-line more. But sometimes the end overshadows the means. We have broken a big psychological barrier by beating the All Blacks."

The next big test was the visit of Australia to HQ seven days later. The world champions were desperate to avoid a third straight defeat to Woodward's troops, but an astonishing second half comeback from 28–16 down saw England come out 32–31 winners with the decisive points coming from, you've guessed it, Jonny Wilkinson!

It was another wonderful display from the Number 10, whose six penalties and two conversions, including one in the last minute, again confirmed his status as the best around.

"It was another too-good-to-be-true display from Wilkinson and his box of tricks," purred Paul Ackford in the *Daily Telegraph* the following day.

At the final whistle, Wilkinson made a beeline for Ben Cohen who had gone over for the last-minute try which won the match, but instead of giving him a pat on the back, the Newcastle fly-half gave him an ear-bashing.

"When Ben scored that try he didn't put the ball down near the posts when he had the chance to. He left me a nasty kick on the left-side which I wasn't best pleased about! Thankfully one of my worst strikes ever went over to make it 32–31."

It wasn't until after the game that anyone realised Wilkinson had made that dramatic last-minute kick in absolute agony. "I had dislocated my finger during the final quarter of the match and the pain was excruciating," he said later. "So there were no handshakes at the end, and I couldn't even lift the trophy. But it's a small price to pay for beating the world champions.

"Coming back from 12 points down was satisfying in the extreme, and to have proved to ourselves that we can cut it when things aren't going our way left everyone smiling in the changing room afterwards. It was one of my greatest experiences in an England shirt."

When the Springboks arrived at Twickenham the following week, England were in the ascendency and red-hot favourites to win on a wintry, but sunny afternoon. However, the South Africans had witnessed Jonny Wilkinson orchestrate England's two victories over the All Blacks and the Wallabies, and were planning on targeting their "jewel in the

In the thick of the action during a man-of-the-match performance against Ireland.

crown" for some very special treatment.

Just 23 minutes into the match, after Wilkinson had again began to boss the midfield, he was taken out by Jannes Labuschagne with a bone-shaking shoulder charge. Labuschagne was instantly red-carded, but it left England's star man battered and bruised.

Wilkinson responded angrily, determined to carry on and help his side overcome the brutal Springboks. But, a quick pick-up pass to Martin Johnson early in the second half resulted in his shoulder 'popping out', and he subsequently left the field to a standing ovation from the crowd. England won the bruising game impressively 53–3, though Wilkinson, who left the ground with his left arm in a sling, was not a happy man.

"I was targetted during the match, of that I have no doubt," Wilkinson said. "There wasn't too much banter between the two teams after the match, I have to admit. I'd be lying if I said that we were rushing to chat to our opponents. It just wasn't that type of match."

Later that week, Wilkinson was quick to put England's undoubted achievements into context. He, like many others, knew that the team had made great strides but he also knew that the three autumn games were friendlies and not games played in the white-hot atmosphere of a World Cup or Six Nations. The side still had to prove they could do it all again when it really mattered.

"It's been a wonderful three weeks but when I walked into the dressing room on Saturday I did so with a massive sense of relief. We must not get carried away. We've had good autumns in the past only to let ourselves down in the Six Nations. We intend to be realistic. Being winners in games that could have gone either way is a sign that we are moving forward but the judgements will only be cast after we've proved that we can also beat these teams away from home," Jonny said.

After nursing his shoulder injury throughout November and December, Wilkinson's focus turned towards 2003. He knew that this was a year that could shape his entire career. It was a year of personal and team destiny. He'd proved that he

was the best player on the planet in his position, but he wanted 2003 to be a year both he and England would never forget. First, the Grand Slam and then the World Cup. One, and not the other wasn't acceptable, but in truth it was the Webb Ellis Trophy he wanted most.

The Queen's New Years Honours list brought Wilkinson his first major recognition outside of the game when he was awarded an MBE. The prestigious award came as a total shock to the modest 23-year old youngster, but nevertheless he went into the 2003 Six Nations tournament a very proud man.

The opening match of the 2003 championship was against the French at Twickenham and Wilkinson knew it was vital. A blustery afternoon greeted the visitors in a game that was billed by pundits as the 'championship decider'. Passions were running high, and before kick-off Wilkinson was as tense as ever. He knew the importance of this game.

Despite the high winds and high nerves, Wilkinson lived up to his own – and England's – expectations, with an impeccable kicking display, scoring 20 of England's 25 points in a tense 25–17 win. Again, Wilkinson's imposing performance had been the difference between the two sides. A fact made even more obvious when you consider that France outscored England by three tries to one. There was only one candidate for man-of-the-match, as Wilkinson took widespread acclaim.

"Well, he's won man-of-the-match before hasn't he?" *The Observer* reporter enthused the next day. "That's what comes of being rugby's all-singing, all-dancing renaissance man. Need a left-footed clearance kick with an ugly back row forward bearing down? Need a right-footed one? Need an ugly back row forward smashed back onto his backside? Will do. Dancing breaks through opposition defence? Cut-out passes the width of the pitch? Pressure place kicks? Match-winning performances? All part of the service."

Even the French were quick to hail the world's best stand-off. Centre Thomas Castaignede said: "We knew how to beat England but we didn't manage to control Wilkinson like we did in Paris last year. Jonny is *the* man. England wouldn't be the same without him. His defence, his running, and when you play against him you have the impression he is everywhere on the pitch. But it is only when you see him on video that you realise how good he is. He is the best in the world."

A week later at a packed Millennium Stadium, England were expected to demolish a Wales team at their lowest ebb after losing to Italy in Rome, but Woodward's men were made to work hard for their win. Despite being well below their best, England ran out comfortable 26–9 winners, with two drop goals, two conversions and two penalties coming from the boot of Wilkinson.

"After the game there was an odd feeling in the dressing room," the Number 10 admitted. "We had won and we had managed to prevent Wales from scoring any tries, but we knew we could have played better. In my personal game, I was frustrated that I made a kicking error early on when going for a penalty. I felt confident generally, but that one took me by surprise. The hardest thing for me when I miss a kick is the knowledge that so much work went into giving me a chance. I don't want to miss those kicks, ever, but I know I have to put it out of my mind and get back into the game quickly."

Between the Wales match and the upcoming game against Italy, Woodward had serious fitness concerns over captain Martin Johnson who was struggling to shake off an Achilles tendon problem. He called young Jonny Wilkinson to his room at the team hotel.

"Clive warned me that if Johnno wasn't involved he'd want to call on me to captain the side," he remembers. "He wanted to know if I was okay with that. I took a few moments to unscramble what he'd just said and then quickly agreed to take on the responsibility. There is no way that I could sleep on it, I couldn't pass up that kind of opportunity. Captaining England was one of those things that I'd dreamed about since playing for Farnham Under-9s.

"Jonno is a great captain who leads by example –

he is more into deeds than words. He never takes a step back and everybody he plays with respects him for that. I know that every word he says is taken seriously by the other players because when I play with him I take him very seriously. He is a good example for me to follow."

Wilkinson rallied his side in a huddle before kick-off and they responded brilliantly by racing into a 33–0 lead within the first 20 minutes. The rest of the game was an anti-climax, as they extended their winning streak at Twickenham to 20 games with a comprehensive 40–5 win. Unfortunately, Wilkinson's dream debut as captain ended prematurely when he left the field two minutes after half-time with a shoulder injury.

After the game, coach Clive Woodward spoke of his delight at the way his star fly-half had coped with his new role: "I thought Jonny did very well. His leadership qualities have been growing game by game and I knew he was ready to step up. He doesn't say a lot off the pitch, but when he talks about rugby, people listen and that's what counts."

Wilkinson himself was philosophical about the premature end to his first experience of international leadership.

"When England were defending I was trying to get hold of the ball to try and turn the game round into attack," he wrote in his *Times* column. "Unfortunately that didn't happen. It was very disappointing to come off injured but it was the right decision because my shoulder was, and still is, very sore. It would have been silly to stay on. As it is, I expect to be back on the field next Saturday.

"After the match, we had a black-tie dinner at the Hilton Hotel, where I made a speech, the first I've made as England captain. It made a great end to one of the most exciting weeks of my life."

England were now just two games away from that elusive Grand Slam, and a passionate Scotland side were the next obstacle in the way. In front of yet another sell-out Twickenham crowd, and back in his familiar role as vice-captain, he produced a masterful display of dead-ball kicking – his trusty left boot scoring 18 valuable points in an easy 40–9 victory. The coach even had the luxury of

being able to rest his star man, taking him off after 66 minutes. After all, the big one was yet to come.

Wilkinson and the team were on their way back to Dublin. One game away from the Grand Slam dream and, just as it had been 17 months earlier, Woodward had to pick a team to beat Ireland at Lansdowne Road. This time, the Irish were in even more buoyant mood as they themselves were on the verge of completing their first Six Nations whitewash for 55 years. It really was winner takes all.

After falling at the final hurdle in 1999, 2000 and 2001, Woodward and his charges were apprehensive about the game. But, those defeats and those heart-breaks had created an inner strength within the squad and Wilkinson was a prime example of that. There was a determination inside his mind that simply wouldn't allow defeat to happen again. Those bad experiences had made him stronger.

"I have always wanted to win a Grand Slam. It's no good pretending it doesn't matter because I am desperate to say that I have got one," he said in his pre-match press conference. "In the last few years we haven't been able to finish it off. It's exhausting when you win four games and then lose the fifth. I use those memories as my force, my incentive when I am out there practising my goalkicking."

He was ready to step up to the plate.

The sun shone on a clear but windy day in Dublin. He awoke to Irish press headlines describing him as "chief choker in a team of bottlers", but that only made the 23-year-old star even more determined to bury his ghosts. He knew he was born to be a winner and this was to be his day.

In the blustery conditions, Wilkinson and England were put under intense early pressure but they stood firm this time and refused to buckle. Rated by former England captain Will Carling as "pound for pound the best tackler in the world", Wilkinson flew into crunching hit after hit like a man possessed. Everywhere you looked, he was there in the thick of the action, dictating the game. England coasted to a 42–6 triumph.

Five minutes from time, as Wilkinson kneeled on the turf to tie his bootlaces, the tannoy announcer revealed that he'd been named man-of-the-match.

Adrenalin was clearly overwhelming his body as the frustration of all those near misses appeared to come out in one super-human performance. A mouth injury halfway through the second-half had forced him off the field for seven minutes, which gave him time to rest the shoulder which was crippling him with pain, but there was no way Wilkinson wasn't going to be on the pitch when the referee blew the final whistle.

His 15 points from two drops, three conversions and a penalty didn't go anywhere near to explaining the quality of his performance.

"Jonny was outstanding today," said Woodward after the game. "The ramifications would have been huge had we lost. It's a very important year with the World Cup at the end of it, and people would have said we could not win away from home if we'd lost. That monkey is off our back."

"Wilkinson was superb," agreed Ireland coach Eddie O'Sullivan. "He had a great service from his pack but he made things happen and he made sure we had to chase the game."

So off Jonny Wilkinson went to enjoy the feeling of being a Grand Slam winner at last. His and the rest of the team's efforts for England since 1998 had been deserving of more than one, but it was truly something to savour when it finally arrived. They had finally shaken off their unwanted tag as 'bottlers' and shown they were now capable of turning their undisputed physical and tactical dominance into consistent results. England had overcome a crucial mental hurdle and, in a World Cup year, the timing could not have been better.

Typically, of course, it was not to be long before Wilkinson's thoughts turned to the World Cup rather than Grand Slam celebrations. England had warm-ups games against the All Blacks and Wallabies to prepare for and he knew the greatest prize of them all was still to be claimed. The English side of 1991 had won the Grand Slam and then gone on to reach the World Cup final, only to fall to Australia. Wilkinson was not going to let history repeat itself. And he knew this time, England would have to go one better than their predecessors thousands of miles from home.

Previous page: Can he kick it? Oh, yes.
Left: Finally, the Grand Slam!

CHAPTER ELEVEN

THE KICK THAT CHANGED THE WORLD

England could not have left for New Zealand and Australia in better heart. The Grand Slam was finally theirs and they had won their last seven games against southern-hemisphere opposition, a feat none of their English predecessors had managed. Now was the time was to prove to their dwindling band of critics that they could beat the best away from home, as well as at Twickenham, and confirm themselves as genuine favourites for the Webb Ellis trophy.

If one doubt still persisted about England, it was their ability to beat New Zealand and Australia, particularly in their own back yard. All of England's three recent wins over the Wallabies had come at Twickenham, and Clive Woodward knew it was almost inconceivable that his side could win the World Cup without having to face Australia or the All Blacks at some point in the knockout stages. England were going to have to acquire the knack of winning Down Under and the two-Test tour was to be their final dress rehearsal.

The clash with the All Blacks proved to be nothing short of an epic encounter.

In atrocious conditions in Wellington, the two teams fought tooth and nail but despite one spell during the second-half when England were reduced to 13 men as Neil Back and Lawrence Dallaglio were condemned to the sin bin, New Zealand could not get their noses in front and England clung on for a famous 15–13 victory. Wilkinson again stole the headlines with all of his team's points from four penalties and a drop goal and the sceptics who had argued that the All Blacks were invincible at home were silenced.

The difficulty of the kicks that Wilkinson slotted safely home in the Wellington wind and rain were almost beyond belief. "Jonny Wilkinson's goal kicking was near miraculous," wrote Paul Ackford in the *Sunday Telegraph*. "His second penalty was so difficult that the ball moved three ways in the air before sailing between the posts. His third, struck into a vicious, blustery wind, was hit from 46 metres and that went through too. And all this on an evening when New Zealand's Carlos Spencer couldn't kick his granny out of bed."

England, inspired by Wilkinson's trusty left boot, had emphatically shrugged off their choker's tag and were the bookie's clear favourites for the World Cup. It was now on to Melbourne and a few old scores that needed settling with the Australians.

And how England settled them as they emerged 25–14 winners with a hugely entertaining performance that left the Australian public gasping in disbelief. The team had been labelled one-dimensional by the local media after their gutsy and dogged display in Wellington, but there could be no doubting their attacking potential now as they scored three beautifully-crafted tries. This time, England did not need Wilkinson's boot to come to the rescue, though he was still on hand to lay the third try on a plate for winger Ben Cohen.

World Cup expectations now went into overdrive. Two famous victories on the eve of the tournament had turned hope to belief and even the pundits from the southern hemisphere began to agree that no-one could stop the English. For Woodward, it was a running battle to keep the hype in check. "This group is very level-headed and and I know we are going to get a lot better," he said. "If we go to the competition as favourites, it's something to be proud of. It's not something we should be scared of. I've deliberately built these two matches into massive pressure games and it seems as if we have a special group of players who

It's all in the preparation…

can handle it. But there are still lots of areas where we can improve. We need to build in a lot more detail. The moment you think you can't improve is the moment you come second."

Back in the UK, the England players, relieved of their club obligations and free to focus solely on the World Cup, continued with their final preparations. Woodward had organised two friendlies with France and another with Wales before finalising his squad for the tournament, but it was to be a quiet time for Wilkinson, who played in just one match as his coach shuffled his options.

The first game took an unfamiliar England side to Cardiff to face a full-strength Wales side and their 43–9 win highlighted the strength in depth Woodward now had at his disposal. A narrow but meaningless 17–16 defeat to France in Marseille followed before Wilkinson was recalled for his 46th cap to what looked like the first-choice England line-up for the return match against France at Twickenham, which was comfortably won 45–14.

England's preparations were finally complete. The team was brimming with confidence and Wilkinson was a different player to the fresh-faced 20-year-old who started the World Cup in 1999 with such hope and expectation. His final date with destiny was set.

It was obvious from the moment that the England plane landed in Australia that the natives were restless. The Australian media had already begun their usual mind games, labelling Clive Woodward's side boring and dangerously over-dependent on Wilkinson's boot, but all the verbal jousting only served to highlight their anxiety. The hosts and defending champions were clearly worried and it was Wilkinson in particular who seemed to be giving their players, press and fans alike the most sleepless nights. England's superb form throughout 2003 in the lead-up to the tournament had not gone unnoticed.

There were signs, however, that the England squad were still a little uncomfortable with their tag of favourites so far from home and as the media interest in the players spiralled almost out of control, a siege mentality within the camp developed. A conscious decision was made that Wilkinson wouldn't give any interviews – rather than agree to some and refuse others – and it seemed like an eternity before Woodward, his coaching team and his players could stop all the talking and get down to the real business in hand.

The waiting finally came to an end on 12 October when England faced the minnows of Georgia, making their debut in the tournament, in their opening group game in Perth's Subiaco Oval. No-one from either side could seriously pretend it was to be a meaningful contest in any sense but Woodward's side were just grateful to get their tracksuits off and their hands dirty. Although they repeatedly and publicly refused to acknowledge it, the team already had one eye on their second group game against the South Africans but first they had to dispatch Georgia.

In the end, it was as one-sided as everyone had predicted as England cruised effortlessly to an 84–6 victory. There was no sense of celebration at the final whistle because all concerned knew the game was nothing more than a stepping stone to bigger and hopefully greater things, but at least England were finally up and running.

And so it was on to the Springboks, England's nemesis in the tournament four years before. True, Woodward's side had won four of their five subsequent clashes with the South Africans since that fateful, Jannie de Beer-inspired day in Paris but there remained a sense of revenge in the air. The winners also knew that they were odds on to take the group and avoid a likely quarter-final clash with New Zealand, as well as probably a semi-final showdown with the Wallabies, which only added to the stakes.

Pre-match predictions of Springbok skullduggery, however, were to prove unfounded. The South African's cynical and often brutal targetting of Wilkinson in England's record-breaking 53–3 win at Twickenham earlier in the year had earned them an unwanted reputation as a dirty side, but the World Cup clash between the two teams in Perth was nothing if not a clean fight.

That England emerged safely with a 25–6 win under their belts would, in a different era, have been more than enough for even their fiercest critics but it was a mark of their new levels of perfection that the performance, if not the result, was greeted with muted applause. "England stumble to nervous victory," ran the headline in the *Daily Telegraph* two days later.

In the end, it was Wilkinson who proved the difference. Although he looked nervous for long phases of the match with the ball in the hand, his kicking was as deadly as ever and he did not miss a single effort at goal as he notched up 20 priceless points. Centre Will Greenwood was England's only other scorer on the day, scoring a try after a Springbok clearance was charged down by Lewis Moody. In contrast, South Africa's outside-half Louis Koen missed four of his six kicks and his team never recovered.

England, however, had failed to convince. The South Africa side was one of their poorest for years and had it not been for Wilkinson's accuracy and Koen's profligacy, the result could have been very different. The first whispers that Woodward's side had peaked in the summer and were too long in the tooth to go all the way could now be heard, albeit emanating chiefly from Australian lips.

If the team hoped to silence their detractors in the next game against the powerful but unpredictable Samoans, they were to be disappointed. England won the match 35–22 but once again the performance raised more questions than it answered. In fact, had it not been for Phil Vickery's try six minutes from the end, the win could still plausibly have gone the other way. The side was winning but not with any real conviction.

The match was also ample evidence that when Wilkinson was off his game, so were England. The fly-half just did not spark on a humid night in the Colonial Stadium in the Australian capital Melbourne, and he looked out of sorts virtually from the first whistle. Surprisingly, he was wayward with four of his kicks at goal and, even more amazingly, he blasted one straightforward, short-range effort against the upright. This just

wasn't the Wilkinson that England fans had come to know and love, and even Woodward was at a loss to explain away his playmaker's poor performance in his post-match press conference. Skipper Martin Johnson was in no mood for excuses though. "That was not good enough," he said afterwards. "Full credit to Samoa. They could have beaten us. We're not going to win anything if we carry on playing like that."

Almost as worrying as Wilkinson's twitchy display was the way the Samoans had been able to get in behind the usually watertight England defence – and the way they shredded it in the sixth minute for Semo Sititi's try was particularly disturbing. England were far from in crisis but, after three matches, they had lost much of the aura they had taken into the start of the tournament.

Predictably, Wilkinson was rested for England's final group game against Uruguay so that he would be fresh for the quarter-finals. Woodward's second string did the job asked of them in some style, beating the south Americans by a thumping 111–13 and setting up a quarter-final clash with old foes Wales in Brisbane. The competition was set to move into the knockout phases and the real action would begin.

Under normal circumstances, few would have given Wales, the 2003 Six Nations whipping boys, a prayer of beating England. Since their famous win over Woodward's side at Wembley in 1999 to deny them the Grand Slam, England had cruised to five straight wins, clocking up a colossal 209 points in the process to Wales' 55. They had got used to giving the Welsh a good hiding. However, with England showing signs of fallibility and Wales encouraged by a vibrant and morale-boosting performance in their group stage defeat to New Zealand, there was actually talk of a Welsh victory.

The game was to be Wilkinson's 50th in England colours but the fly-half had little time for sentimentality in the build-up. It was, he insisted just another game and the result and nothing else mattered. Luckily for England, the man who refused to celebrate his international half century was absolutely right.

Wales came at England in the first half of Suncorp Stadium like men possessed, and courtesy of tries from Stephen Jones and captain Colin Charvis, led 10–3 at the break. It was time for Wilkinson to steady the ship and he did so with trademark nervelessness – slotting five second-half penalties and a crisply-struck 40-metre drop goal in the dying seconds to steer his side to a 28-17 win and, more importantly, a place in the semi-finals against France. Wales, the underdogs, took the plaudits but it was England heading to the last four and, they hoped, beyond.

With Wilkinson back to his peerless best with the boot, his detractors, who seemed ever more bent on finding some way of unsettling him, singled out his appetite to go looking for tackles, as well as his tendency to get involved in a high number of rucks and mauls, as a cause for concern. Woodward, though, was having none of it. "He plays like a wing forward so you do need someone to step into the Number 10 role to cover. But I don't want to change the way that Jonny operates. He's been like that since I've known him. Why would you want to change him? The team have got to adapt to him."

England's thoughts turned to the French who, in contrast to Woodward's team, had enjoyed trouble-free progress through to the semi-finals, winning the praise of the purists with their typically elegant and expansive performances.

In the process, their young fly-half Frederic Michalak had stylishly emerged in some people's eyes as the star Number 10 of the tournament ahead of Wilkinson, and suddenly England's stand-off had lost his crown. Yet again, he would have to justify his big reputation.

The contrast in England and France's build-up to the semi-final was stark. France appeared to spend almost the whole week relaxing very publicly on Bondi Beach while England seemed tense and edgy both on and off the training pitch. The bookmakers slashed their odds on the French, and even England fans began to wonder whether Woodward and his men were going to be able to handle the anticipated Gallic onslaught that lay ahead of them.

Wilkinson seemed to be carrying the weight of the world on his shoulders as the semi-final drew close and, in a press conference during the week, he was bombarded by questions about whether he was happy with his own form. "I just want to put the effort in and just try to make the right decisions," he said in his defence. "I'm still looking at the video tapes and keeping in tune with my memories of games, knowing I could have done things differently. I wouldn't say I have a corner to turn nor would I say I'm playing well. It's somewhere in between. There is a pressure, it's pressure I put on myself but I would put the same pressure on myself if I was in another profession."

But as ever, the talking had to come to a stop and actions were to speak louder than words as Wilkinson and England finally crossed swords with Michalak and France. In the end, there was to be only one winner in Sydney's Telstra Stadium.

The conditions were typically northern rather than southern hemisphere as the heavens opened and it was to be England who adapted best to the downpour. The French took the lead in the 10th minute through a try from flanker Serge Betsen after endless reviews by the video referee and although Michalak converted from wide out, it was to be France's first and last score of the whole match. It was now Wilkinson's turn to bask in the limelight.

In the end, England did not score a try during the entire 80 minutes but Wilkinson's five penalties and three drop goals – two in the first-half – were more than enough to lead his side to a 24-7 victory. The young Michalak had dismally failed to live up to his pre-match billing and was a forlorn figure when substituted just after the hour. England had regained their old swagger and Wilkinson was reinstalled as the world's number one after scoring all of his team's points. It had been a job well and truly done.

"At the back of everyone's minds, this was the game that we had been waiting for," Woodward said. "Last Tuesday we had a meeting and there was a lot of bad-natured anger from the coaches and a lot of good-natured anger from the players

One game away from destiny: Jonny on the rampage in the semi-final against France.

when we saw the tapes of the Wales game. We handled it well."

Woodward's opposite number, French coach Bernard Laporte was gracious in defeat, even if he could not resist a swipe at those who had foolishly written off England's all-conquering fly-half before the game.

"We were very edgy and fragile when it mattered," he said. "The blame has to be at our own door. It's too easy to take refuge in the weather. It was the same for England but they showed flexibility and we did not. The better team won, that is for sure.

"They tell me that Wilkinson is dead. Well, he didn't look dead. He played a great match. You saw the difference today with Freddie Michalak."

The stage was now set. England had made the final and a nation was expectant. All that stood between them and glory were the hosts and defending champions Australia. The Wallabies, who had broken All Black hearts in their own semi-final epic, were not going to surrender their crown without one hell of a fight. Especially not to the Poms.

The build-up to the final, the reverse psychology and the anti-Wilkinson campaign by the Australian media made the week before the match almost as enthralling as the game itself. If the Aussies had been nervous about the English fly-half's match-winning abilities before the tournament, they were now positively terrified.

The host nation's attempts to unsettle England ranged from the bizarre to the ridiculous. One newspaper was quick to label Woodward as "the manager of the bored" in reference to his side's allegedly limited game plan, while the governor of New South Wales ordered that the Sydney Opera House, normally resplendent in white, should be immediately decked out in the green and gold of the Wallabies lest anyone think he was being unpatriotic. Radio stations the length and breadth of the country vowed to play 'Waltzing Matilda' constantly three hours before kick-off on match day. If they had ever been in any doubt, Wilkinson and company know knew they were going to have

take on the entire country, mentally if not physically, if they wanted to come home with any the trophy.

But the prize for the most paranoid, and in turn most revealing, stunt in the days before the final must surely go to the *Sydney Daily Telegraph*, which decided that Wilkinson represented such a threat to Australian hopes that it printed a cut-out voodoo doll of the England fly-half. It urged their readers to stick pins in various bits of his anatomy whenever he lined up a kick. "With a little luck," ran the paper's editorial, "Jonny will be out of commission in the early moments and you will have played a role in his demise and share Wallaby glory." It was all done with tongues firmly in cheeks, but the sense of fear Wilkinson was inspiring was obvious. Australians were not used to finding themselves in awe of a Pom.

The attempted wind-ups, however, did not seem to upset England. If they had been tense and withdrawn for much of the tournament, never more so than in the build-up to the French game, they now seemed reborn and relaxed. They had come to contest the final and, having reached it, they appeared at peace with themselves.

Woodward, in particular, was the model of calm reassurance. "There is nothing I would change going into this game in the selection or the training," he said, "and that gives you a certain amount of inner confidence. But we have to keep our feet firmly on the ground and take away the hype and treat it just like any other game of rugby."

His team selection was certainly consistent, with the only change from the side that saw off the French being the return of Mike Tindall in the midfield for Mike Catt. Catt had done nothing wrong in the semi-final but Woodward was mindful of the physical presence of Wallaby centre Stirling Mortlock, who had a barnstorming game against New Zealand in the semi-final, and the equally abrasive Tindall was drafted back in to snuff out the danger. It was to prove a wise decision.

The final, held in Sydney's impressive Telstra Stadium, was played on the evening of 22 November 2003, Australia versus England. It was a night that ebbed and flowed with drama and

Holding on in the face of fierce Australian pressure.

emotion and it was also a night that lasted longer than most had expected. There were to be no short-cuts to glory this evening.

The early exchanges between the two sets of forwards were predictably fierce as both teams looked to build a platform but it was the hosts who drew first blood courtesy of Lote Tuqiri's try.

It was time for Wilkinson to make his first real contribution of the game, slotting penalties in the 12th and 19th minutes – the first a monster just five metres short of the halfway – to give his team a slender 6–5 advantage. The England fly-half added a third kick on 28 minutes to extend the lead and with time before the turnaround running out, it seemed that Woodward and his side would have to content themselves with a four-point cushion.

They had not, however, reckoned on the twinkling feet of Robinson. From the breakdown, Lawrence Dallaglio, like Wilkinson a great player too quickly maligned during the early stages of the tournament, made an arching break, taking out two Wallaby tacklers before offloading to the supporting Wilkinson. With the Australian line beckoning, Wilkinson weighed up his options before delivering the decisive pass to Robinson on his left who out-paced the cover to slide in at the corner. England had the boost of a try at a psychologically important time and went in 14–5 in front.

Australia were down but not out and they knew it was vital that they scored first after the break, which they did on 47 minutes as England fluffed another lineout and conceded a penalty – which Flatley stroked over. He repeated the dose on the hour after a moment of madness from Phil Vickery and the score stood tantalisingly at 14–11 to the visitors. Who would hold their nerve?

In the end it was to be the Australians. In the final minute of normal time, England once again made a mess of their own lineout ball and, from the resulting scrum, conceded a penalty. Flatley stepped forward and, with unbelievable calmness and his country's hopes resting on his shoulders, he kicked the three points.

The final would go into extra-time.

If England were stunned by the dogged Australian fightback, they did not show it. With just two minutes gone, they presented Wilkinson with a 47 metre penalty chance. His effort crept over the crossbar and England were back in the lead.

The next 15 minutes saw are no further scores – thanks in no small part to a heroic tackle from Robinson on Tuqiri with the England line in sight – and Woodward's side knew if they could just keep the Wallabies out for another three minutes, they would be world champions. But Dallaglio conceded a penalty 25 metres out and Flatley, once again displayed almost superhuman cool, held his nerve to take the chance and level the scores at 17 apiece with little more than two minutes left on the clock. Sudden death loomed unless someone could conjure up one final score. It was time for Wilkinson's date with destiny.

Although it will be Wilkinson who is forever remembered for what followed, it is important to pay tribute to the team-mates who made it possible: Substitute flanker Lewis Moody won a line-out in the Australian 22, Mike Catt blasted up the middle and England recycled the ball back to scrum-half Matt Dawson at the breakdown.

At this point, everyone in the stadium, not to mention the millions watching on television around the world, were expecting the inevitable drop goal attempt from the England Number 10 but Dawson opted for a quick dart on the open side which bought his side priceless yards and forced the Australians onto the back foot. Yet again England retained possession, skipper Martin Johnson took the ball up for one last time and the rest of the England side could do no more. There were only 20 seconds left on the clock.

It was now all about Wilkinson.

As Dawson fired out the pass to his half-back partner, the crowd went silent. Wilkinson safely collected the ball as the Wallaby defence desperately scrambled towards him, dropped his shoulder and unleashed a sweetly-struck right-foot drop goal that sailed handsomely through the posts. England had won the World Cup and Wilkinson's life would never be the same again.

Previous page: *That* kick. Left: A well-deserved pat on the head from Matt Dawson before the trophy presentation.

CHAPTER TWELVE

THE BEST OF TIMES... THE WORST OF TIMES

It is hard to measure the impact England's World Cup triumph in Sydney had on the national psyche. For so long rugby had played second fiddle to football, occasionally grabbing the headlines only to politely step aside once again and now suddenly it was the only subject of conversation. England had been yearning for a reason to celebrate, to unite behind a sporting side that could call themselves world champions and Clive Woodward's team had provided them with what they wanted in dramatic, iconic style.

England went rugby mad. When the squad's flight back from Australia touched down at Heathrow on a cold, grey November morning, they were greeted by thousands of delirious fans who braved the elements to salute the returning heroes. The players were suddenly being treated more like pop stars rather than sportsmen and if they thought their reception at the airport was extraordinary, they were in for a shock. The national adulation was only just beginning.

Such was the need to acknowledge the team's achievement that an open top bus ride through London was hastily organised and the incredible 750,000 people who thronged the streets to cheer the players spoke volumes of the country's mood. Receptions at Downing Street and Buckingham Street followed and the England rugby team justifiably basked in the glory.

And at the centre of it all, albeit reluctantly, was Wilkinson. The pin-up boy, the man who dropped that goal, the talisman of the team, Wilkinson was feted wherever he went. His innate modesty and obvious desire to shun the limelight only served to fuel the frenzied interest in the 24-year-old and his face stared back at him from countless newspapers, magazines and television pro-grammes. The country was suffering from an acute bout of Jonny mania.

There was yet more to come. A mere 48 hours after his first visit with royalty, Wilkinson was back at Buckingham Palace to collect an MBE from the Queen for his services to rugby. The fact he had been involved in a minor car crash the day before on his way home to Newcastle couldn't stop collecting his gong and he was, of course, predictably self-effacing when asked about the occasion.

"I told the Queen she sounded like my mum," he confessed. "She asked me how I was. I said I was fine and that it was a very, very minor crash. When she gave me the MBE, the Queen said how much she had enjoyed the reception earlier in the week. We're all still talking about it – to be here twice in a week is just a fantastic honour. It's something I'm never going to forget."

The world was now at his feet but typically he refused to be seduced by the plaudits, the adulation and his new-found status as a genuine national hero. Rugby was to remain his first and foremost love. "I won't be distracted," he insisted. "Any commercial projects that interfere with my rugby get binned. Ten years, after I've retired, when people are sitting around the pub discussing their dream, all-time XV, I want to be in there. Or at least, if not in the final line-up, I want to be in their deliberations. You want your reputation to carry on after you're finished."

The young fly-half could have been forgiven for yearning for a well-earned rest after his exertions Down Under and unfortunately he was about to be forced to take one. Within a fortnight of his match-winning performance against Australia, Wilkinson was diagnosed with a broken facet in

Top: Wilkinson lines up with the 2005 British & Irish Lions squad.
Bottom: Jonny faces the media on tour with the Lions

his shoulder and what was to be a four-year injury nightmare had begun. Already capped 52 times by his country, the number 10 would wait a soul-destroying 1,169 days before he pulled on the white shirt of England again.

The shoulder injury had forced him to sit out the 2004 Six Nations campaign and he was also conspicuous by his absence when England set out that summer for a tour of Australia and New Zealand. The team was in transition and without Wilkinson's calming influence, they went down heavily in Australia and also lost the two-Test series against the All Blacks.

When the 2004–05 season began, it seemed that Wilkinson had been able to put his injury problems behind him. New England head coach Andy Robinson – who had succeeded Clive Woodward – decided to select Jonny as captain for the autumn internationals.

"It's the ambition of so many players to one day be captain of England and today I have realised a dream," Wilkinson said when the news was announced. "I'm honoured Andy wants me to be his captain, and to follow Lawrence [Dallaglio] and Martin [Johnson] means a lot to me as they are inspirational men who have given so much to England rugby over many years.

"Getting my first England cap against Ireland six years ago was something I'll never forget because to play for your country is very special. Taking on the captaincy is another important step in my career and I do so with immense pride."

His elation was to prove frustratingly short lived. A ruptured blood vessel in his upper right arm forced back into the treatment room and Jason Robinson assumed the captaincy. The 2005 Six Nations was his next target and just as it seemed he had recovered from the haematoma, he damaged medial knee ligaments in a club clash for Newcastle against French side Perpignan. His injury problems seemed to be turning into a fully-fledged jinx. These were dark times. It was 18 months since England had lifted the Webb Ellis Trophy and ever since that famous night in

Sydney, Wilkinson had suffered nothing but bad luck. For a man who lived to play rugby, the enforced periods of inactivity were torture.

There was, however, one bright spot on the horizon. The British & Irish Lions were scheduled to tour New Zealand in the summer of 2005 and with Woodward, his old England coach, at the helm, Wilkinson had something to aim for. All he had to was prove his fitness. Woodward announced his initial 44-man squad in April and although Wilkinson's name was not on the list, the message was relayed that if he could get a few games under his belt for the Falcons, the situation would be reviewed. The fly-half did exactly that and when the final touring party was unveiled in May, Wilkinson's name was there for all to see. It may not have been a return to the fray for his beloved England but he was about to step foot on the international stage again.

"It is great to have him back in form and playing well," said Lions captain Brian O'Driscoll. "Mentally he is a tough player, his skill level is as high as you can get and he is the complete number 10. He's an incredibly organised individual. He's got a clear idea of what he wants, he's very structured, he's a very confident guy. He is just so good at what he does."

For the man himself, his last-minute call-up was a huge relief. The 2001 Lions tour to Australia and the series defeat still lingered in his mind and now he had the opportunity to make amends. His selection had seemed an impossible dream six months earlier but his sheer, stubborn willpower had seen him through and he was poised to renew acquaintances with the famed All Blacks.

However there was one problem: the Lions number 10 shirt seemed destined for fly-half Stephen Jones, the man who had just orchestrated Wales' 2005 Six Nations Grand Slam success. Jones was on the top of his game while Wilkinson had played so little competitive rugby and despite Woodward having shown great faith in picking his former England charge, there was no way he could overlook the Welshman.

Wilkinson is tackled by two All Blacks in the first Test in Christchurch

"If I'm not good enough to be in the team, I'm sure I won't be picked," was Wilkinson's disarmingly honest assessment of the situation. "It's about going out and helping the squad the best I can. Everyone has a huge part to play out there whether or not they play in the Tests. Physically I'm fit and I'm working hard. I'm enthusiastic and ready to get out there."

Ironically, Wilkinson's long-awaited international comeback came in Cardiff rather than Canterbury or Christchurch. The Lions has organised a one-off warm-up game with Argentina at the Millennium Stadium, Cardiff, before they flew to New Zealand and Woodward, mindful of the need to give Wilkinson precious game time, named in his starting line-up.

Most of the match itself was an instantly forgettable affair in which the Lions fluffed their lines alarmingly, but what did live in the memory after the final whistle was Wilkinson's contribution. The fly-half showed no signs of his long lay-off and his six penalties – including a glorious last-minute touchline effort and one conversion – earned Woodward's side a face-saving 25–25 draw in Cardiff. Eighteen months after slaying the Wallabies, he was back in Test match rugby.

The Lions headed to New Zealand acutely aware that the All Blacks, the number one ranked side in the world, were lurking with intent. Still licking their wounds in the wake of the World Cup, the Kiwis had a point to prove and a series victory over the tourists would be the perfect way of proving it.

As the first Test in Christchurch in late June loomed, Woodward sprung a major selection surprise. As predicted, Jones was named as fly-half but Wilkinson was also included in the team and would partner O'Driscoll in the Lions midfield. Woodward, it seemed, just could not bring himself to leave him out.

The game in the Jade Stadium was played in atrocious conditions and the tone for the tourists was set in the first minute when O'Driscoll was stretchered off with a dislocated shoulder after a horrendous spear tackle by Keven Mealamu and Tana Umaga. The Lions had lost their skipper and the game was not far behind. The All Blacks tore into the opposition with a real ferocity and tries either side of the break from Ali Williams and Sitiveni Sivivatu sealed the Lions' fate. Wilkinson landed a second-half penalty but it was too little, too late and New Zealand recorded a convincing 21–3 win.

It was a chastening experience for all of the squad and with just a week to prepare for the second Test in Wellington, there was little time to put things right. Woodward decided to be bold in his team selection and made wholesale changes but the most significant (and debated) was his decision to drop Jones to the bench and restore Wilkinson to fly-half. The England star was back in the driver's seat.

New Zealand however had not finished with their Lion-hunt. The defeat in Christchurch was heavy, but the loss which followed in Wellington was catastrophic. The All Blacks produced 80 minutes of unstoppable attacking rugby that simply blew away the Lions. Wilkinson contributed eight points with the boot but he was, for once, eclipsed by his opposite number Dan Carter who scored two tries in an eventual 48–18 mauling.

Wilkinson is helped off the pitch after suffering a 'stinger' injury in the second Test at Wellington

The final scoreline was bad enough but the sight of Wilkinson being helped from the pitch in the second-half was terrible. The fly-half suffered a neck and shoulder injury – a 'stinger' – while tackling Carter and he could play no further part in the game. His injury problems had returned to haunt him.

"Jonny got two bangs on the same piece of nerve," Lions doctor James Robson said after the game. "Since then, he's made fantastic progress. If this tour had two weeks to run, then no doubt he'd be available for selection next week. It is a bruising to some of the nerves coming out of the neck and going into the shoulder. Jonny will recover very quickly. The first one cleared very quickly in a few seconds, and the second one was of sufficient concern to actually bring him out of that danger area. It can take anything between a few moments or many months."

This time there was to be no miracle recovery. With the series lost, Woodward refused to consider Wilkinson for the final Test in Auckland and his tour was over. He had overcome the odds to make the trip but injury had once again got the better of him. Sadly, it was the start of another prolonged period on the sidelines.

The stinger healed but on Newcastle's pre-season tour of Japan in August 2005 he was struck down by an appendicitis. In November, he went under the surgeon's knife for a hernia and in February, he suffered an abductor muscle injury. A medial ligament tear in February the following year and a lacerated kidney in November 2006 further compounded the misery.

His luck finally changed in 2007. With his litany of injuries finally forgotten, new England coach Brian Ashton named Wilkinson in his squad for the upcoming Six Nations campaign. He had yet to make his comeback in Newcastle colours but so alarming was England's recent form – a slump that coast Andy Robinson his job – Ashton was willing to gamble on the team's talisman. Wilkinson was of course reluctant to talk up chances of playing for his country once more.

"Who knows, maybe one day I will get to move that next step up the ladder and play for England again," he wrote in *The Times*. "It was a surprise for me to get called back to the England squad. I'm a work in progress and unlikely to warrant selection for the start of the Six Nations campaign."

Ashton had other ideas and duly picked him to face Scotland in the first game at Twickenham in early February. He had last played for England in November 2003 but as he stepped out onto the Twickenham pitch and now, 1,169 days later, he was an England player again.

It was if he had never been away. Scotland were put to the sword and Wilkinson was executioner-in-chief. England scored 42 points – a full house of a try, two conversions, five penalties and a trade-mark drop-goal – to set a new individual Calcutta Cup points record of 27. It was a fairytale return and earned him the man of the match award. Italy in Rome were next in the firing line and his personal haul of 15 points in England's 20–7 victory to become the highest points scorer in the history of the Championship. The records were tumbling as they had before his injury nightmare and with the World Cup in France later in the year looming, England's prospects of defending their crown had suddenly and unexpectedly brightened.

Wilkinson's performance was one of the few positives to be taken from England's 43–13 mauling at Croke Park by Ireland in the next game and although he was forced to sit out the tournament climax with a niggling cramp problem, there was to be no long-term lay-off and he was fit to tour with England for a two-Test series against the Springboks in the summer. Ashton's second string side were badly beaten in both games but Wilkinson at least came through unscathed and he featured in all three of England's World Cup warm-up games against Wales and the French.

The stage was now set for the World Cup. It was to be his third assault on the tournament and even though England had been written off even before they set foot in France, he was ready. He had endured a series of injuries that would have ended the careers of some players but he was now fit and raring to go.

CHAPTER THIRTEEN

HERO JONNY RESTORES ENGLAND'S PRIDE

England arrived in France for their defence of the World Cup in late August and before a ball had even been kicked or a tackle made in the tournament, Brian Ashton's side had been written off. Deprived of Wilkinson's services, England's downward spiral since their triumph in Sydney four years earlier had been spectacular and even with their talismanic fly-half back in the ranks, no one gave England a prayer of retaining their title as world champions.

The consensus of opinion was the English would struggle to reach the semi-finals and some sceptics even suggested they could fail to make the knock-out stages at all. Never before in the history of the competition had the defending champions been so universally dismissed as also-rans before a single match had been played.

Wilkinson, however, was simply relieved just to be there. In the four years following his famous drop kick against the Wallabies, there were serious doubts whether he would ever pull on an England shirt again and to be afforded the chance to play at another World Cup was a minor miracle. The 28-year-old had learnt to count his blessings since the last tournament and it was a relaxed, more mature and less obsessive player who flew to France with the rest of the England squad to defend their crown.

England were drawn in Pool A of the competition with South Africa, the United States of America, Tonga and Samoa. The form book said it would be the Springboks and Ashton's side vying for top spot and a more favourable quarter-final draw. England would take on the South Africans in Paris in their second group game but first they had to beat the Americans and get their campaign off to a winning start.

Wilkinson was poised to win his 61st cap but on the Tuesday before the game disaster struck. The England squad were running through their defensive drills when the fly-half twisted his ankle and went down in agony. The England medical team surrounded the player but the damage had been done and they confirmed he had an ankle ligament sprain. Ashton named his side to face the USA later that day and it was Bath's Olly Barkley and not Wilkinson who was named at fly-half. The injury jinx had struck again.

"This weekend is out, against the United States, we all know that, but after that it is totally open," he wrote in *The Times*. "I am going day by day and there is a realistic chance that thereafter anything – and by that I mean playing in the South Africa game – is possible.

"After all the recent years of injury frustration, it does seem a little unfair that my name should again be on the injury list, and on only day one of our World Cup campaign. Yet while there have been plenty of dark times as I have battled through injuries, this is not one of them."

England were to feel his absence acutely. Against the Americans in Lens in their opener, the champions were embarrassingly pedestrian against a team that was expected to offer little resistance and the final scoreline of 28–10 seemed only to confirm the gloomy pre-tournament view that England's involvement in France would not be prolonged.

Despite his optimistic diagnosis, Wilkinson's ankle injury did not heal in time for the crunch clash with the Springboks. He was nearing full fitness but the South Africa game came too soon and Ashton had to prepare a side for the game at the Stade de France without his best player. The

A sidelined Jonny Wilkinson watches glumly from the stands during the early Pool A matches

coach's woes were intensified when Barkley was ruled out with a hip injury and he was forced to turn to veteran Mike Catt to play at number ten.

England fans were desperately hoping the anaemic performance against the USA would prove to be nothing more than a blip but it quickly became obvious against the Springboks that the team's problems ran deep.

The game in Paris was arguably England's worst Test match display for 20 years. South Africa scored their first try through flanker Juan Smith after just six minutes and the next 74 minutes were an unmitigated hell for the players, Ashton and the fans as the Springboks demolished England in every department of the game and emerged 36–0 winners. England had not even troubled the scorers and the defeat was as comprehensive as it was soul destroying. England's motto going into the tournament had been 'Shock The World' and the critics were quick to point out that was exactly what they had done in Paris.

"This was a record margin of defeat on the global stage," wrote Robert Kitson in *The Guardian*. "At this rate, the erstwhile world champions can expect to be out of the tournament by next Saturday."

England's chances of reaching the quarter-finals were now hanging by a thread. Defeat to either Samoa or Tonga would send England home early and there was now absolutely no margin for error.

The mood in the England camp following the debacle against South Africa was initially bleak but it was not all doom and gloom. Wilkinson was now back in full training and his ankle appeared to have healed with remarkable speed. The hero was of 2003 was poised to make his bow in 2007 against Samoa and he for one was convinced England could turn things around and make an impact on the tournament.

"The South Africa game now needs to be the final straw, the hardest lesson and the final one," he told *The Times*. "It is one thing to lose when you have given your all and played to your best; defeat on those terms hurts, but you can accept it.

But so far we have not come remotely close to giving our best, we have hardly had a glimpse of it."

England made the perfect start against Samoa at the Stade de la Beaujoire in Nantes. A charged down kick saw Wilkinson in possession after just two minutes and he fired out a pass to skipper Martin Corry, who spun out of the tackle to score. Wilkinson added the conversion and England could breathe a tentative sigh of relief. Three minutes later he added a drop goal and Ashton's side were already 10 points clear.

It was, in truth, proving to be a fairytale comeback for the Newcastle fly-half. His grubber kick for wing Paul Sackey set up the second try and he kept the Samoans at arm's length with some astute tactical kicking. Two second-half penalties and another drop goal ensured England were never in danger of being beaten, eventually running out convincing 44–22 winners. Their World Cup dream was still very much alive.

"Wilkinson really punished us," admitted Samoa coach Michael Jones. "It's good to see him back. The whole world respects Jonny. He's all class. He's such a perfectionist and did not shy from tackling even when we sent Henry Tuilagi at him a few times."

Although he uncharacteristically missed two penalties, Wilkinson's personal haul of 24 points made him only the third player in rugby history to pass the 1,000 points in Test matches – behind Wales' Neil Jenkins and Italy's Diego Dominguez – and also moved him above Australia's Michael Lynagh into second place in the list of the all-time World Cup points scorers. He had scored 206 points in three tournaments and now had Scotland's Gavin Hastings (227) firmly in his sights. The records however mattered little to him. What was more important was that England were back on track and their destiny remained in their own hands.

The final group game against Tonga was played at the Parc des Princes in Paris. The Pacific Islanders had given South Africa an almighty scare in their last match and they knew that if they could topple Ashton's side, it would be them and

Back in action, Wilkinson tries to break through the Samoan defence

not England heading to the quarter-finals. The stakes could not have been higher.

Worryingly, Tonga were the first to score in the French capital. After just eight minutes, Mark Cueto conceded a penalty when he was caught in possession inside his own 22 and Tongan fly-half Pierre Hola stepped up to accept the three points on offer. England needed a steadying hand and Wilkinson provided it. Tonga were penalised for handling in a ruck and the fly-half duly landed the resulting penalty to level the scores.

English nerves were frayed when Sukanaivalu Hufanga crashed over for the first try of the match but Wilkinson hit back minutes later to ensure the team stayed in touch. England were awarded a penalty and Tonga assumed Wilkinson would kick for goal but the number ten had other ideas and launched a pinpoint cross-field kick which wing Paul Sackey gleefully collected to score. A drop goal, another penalty and a second Sackey try put England into the lead and Ashton's team went into the dressing room at half-time holding a precious 19–10 lead.

As they had done in the first period, it was Tonga who scored first after the break with a Hola penalty but when Matthew Tait got England's third try after 53 minutes, the result was never in doubt again. Andy Farrell got the fourth try with a quarter of an hour still on the clock and although the Tongans scored a late consolation try, England were home and dry.

"We did the basics right but it was a tough," Wilkinson admitted after the team's 36–20 win. "We became strong at the end. To win by a few points is satisfying – but we've a fair way to go. I still need to improve, most of the stuff in my head is what I need to improve upon.

"It's a fantastic result for us to be where we are at the moment. I think a few weeks ago it was looking pretty tough for us in the pool phase, with two games to go and two games to win and against guys clearly showing that they can play some serious rugby. To come here and win, we are over the moon with that."

England had avoided the humiliation of being the first defending champions to fail to reach the

quarter-finals. They had picked themselves up after their Springbok mauling and although neither the performance against Tonga nor the one against Samoa was perfect, the team was at least improving. The swagger England had in 2003 would be hard to recapture but they were through to the last eight and anything could happen.

"I'm delighted for the players that the game was won," Ashton said. "Firstly, it was a knockout game, so to win that was pleasing. Secondly, we scored a bonus point with four tries, but we know we didn't put in a perfect performance. Two weeks ago, according to a lot of people, we were down and out in the tournament. But we're through to the knock-out stages. We know we'll have to go up a gear at least next Saturday."

England's reward for victory over Tonga was a quarter-final clash with Australia in Marseille, a repeat of the 2003 final. It had been four years since Wilkinson had driven a stake through Australian hearts in the Telstra Stadium with one dramatic, iconic strike with his right foot and although the two teams were much changed in

terms of personnel, the Wallabies finally had their chance for revenge.

The game in the Stade Velodrome was a sellout and the tension was unbelievable as Wilkinson kicked off to get the match started but it was Australia who drew first blood after six minutes when captain Stirling Mortlock landed a penalty. The lead lasted for 15 minutes until England clawed their back into contention when the Wallabies were penalised for offside and Wilkinson accepted the three points on offer.

By this stage, England's pack were beginning to get on top of the Australians and there was tangible reward for their increasing dominance after 24 minutes when the Wallabies were whistled for collapsing a scrum. Wilkinson landed the penalty to ensure the pack's efforts were not wasted and despite the pre-match predictions that England could not beat Australia, it was now obvious it was going to be a titanic encounter.

With half-time approaching, the men in gold stepped up the tempo and England found themselves on the back foot. A succession of attacks

Jonny does more than stop the dangerous Australian centre Matt Giteau;
he tries to steal the ball from him during the quarter-final in Marseille

stretched the defence to breaking point and it finally gave way when wing Lote Tuqiri burst through Josh Lewsey's despairing tackle for a try, as he had done in the final four years earlier. Mortlock added the conversion and Australia were 10–6 to the good at half-time.

The England team of earlier in the tournament would probably have wilted under the pressure at this stage but the side had a new-found steel that ran from one to 15 and they emerged for the second-half with a grim look of determination etched on their faces.

Wilkinson's third penalty on 51 minutes after Australia were caught offside cut the gap to a single point and they took the lead nine minutes later when the scrum demolished Australia once again and Rocky Elsom was penalised. Wilkinson drew a deep breath, clasped his hands together as he had done a thousand times before and sent his kick sailing through the posts.

Against all the odds, England were 12–10 up. The clock was ticking and Australia were desperate to avoid another defeat at the hands of their old enemy but whatever the Wallabies threw at them, Ashton's side repelled them. Their one chance fell to Mortlock but his 45-metre penalty attempt from near the touchline sailed agonisingly wide of the post. England were through to the semi-finals of the World Cup.

Victory had been forged by England's forwards and although the headlines predictably saluted Wilkinson's match-winning contribution, the fly-half was the first to salute the foundations laid by his team-mates.

"That immense effort from the pack is what rugby teams are all about," he wrote in *The Times*. "In the second half, when we were defending, scrambling around in the backs, making huge efforts to stop Australia getting that second try. That is what makes us proud to be together. We have had to come a long way very quickly and it is a great feeling.

"There's certainly a lot to be proud of. It was a real joy to be part of. One of the best days of my life. What I have particularly relished is the way everyone has attacked the whole campaign since the South Africa match. The pressure the team was under then was huge and the honesty, the feeling and the desire that drove us forward from that point on has been phenomenal."

Wilkinson had become the highest scorer in World Cup history with his 12 points against the Australians but he knew an epic quarter-final had been won by the men up front.

England's victory over the Australians was not the only seismic shock to reverberate through the quarter-final stages. Hosts France played New Zealand in Cardiff later the same day and if the rugby fraternity had been surprised by England's triumph, they were struck dumb by Les Bleus' win over the All Blacks. The Kiwis had been the red hot favourites to win the World Cup but they were dramatically ambushed by the French at the Millennium Stadium and England would face Bernard Laporte's side in the semi-final in Paris rather than Graham Henry's team.

Brian Ashton was able to name an unchanged XV for the match, with Jason Robinson set to win his 50th cap for his country, but much of the pre-match debate focused on the battle between the two sets of forwards. England, it was argued, would not be able to bully the French pack in the same way that they had the Australians and the majority of neutral observers made France clear favourites to progress to the final.

"We need to go up a gear and improve in all areas," said skipper Phil Vickery before the game. "We are playing the host nation in their home stadium, they are going to have the crowd behind them. France are an extremely difficult team to play against but we can go into Saturday with confidence."

England had not won in Paris since 2000 but their chances of ending their barren run were given an almost immediate boost in the Stade de France. Les Bleus kicked off to a tumultuous roar from the crowd but a mere 78 seconds later England had scored the first try. Andy Gomarsall's box kick bounced fiendishly inside the French 22 and with full-back Damien Traille unsure how to deal with the threat, Josh Lewsey pounced on the loose ball and crashed through Traille's tackle to score in the corner. Wilkinson missed the difficult conversion attempt, but England had drawn first blood and the eagerly-anticipated cross-Channel clash was well and truly underway.

France may have been rocked by England's early score but they were not down. Wilkinson's opposite number, young Lionel Beauxis, reduced the arrears on eight minutes with a penalty after Nick Easter was caught offside and Les Bleus were in front midway through the half when Beauxis added another three points. It had already become a war of attrition between the two sets of forwards and with although only 20 minutes had elapsed, it was already evident to most of the capacity crowd and the millions watching around the world that there would be little to separate the two sides at the final whistle.

Wilkinson had to call on all his experience to marshal the England effort and he lead from the front, inflicting such a crunching tackle on France second row veteran Fabein Pelous that he was forced off the pitch. Neither side was taking any prisoners.

There were no further scores before the break and the second-half followed the same brutal pattern of the first and it was France who extended their lead four minutes after the restart. Easter was penalised for coming in from the side at a ruck and Beauxis landed his third penalty. England however resisted the temptation to panic and four minutes later Wilkinson contributed his first points of the game with a penalty to make it a one-point match once again. Les Bleus were ahead but England were breathing down their necks. The next 25 minutes saw no further scores and with just five minutes on the clock in Paris, the semi-final hung tantalisingly in the balance.

It was the French who finally cracked. Jason Robinson took the ball up and replacement hooker Dimitri Szarzewski committed the cardinal sin of conceding a penalty within Wilkinson's range after he was blown up for a high tackle on the England full-back. Wilkinson placed the ball

30 metres out, the crowd went quiet and he delivered a kick that sailed safely through the posts. The massive English contingent in the Stade de France erupted in celebration and Ashton's side were 11–9 in front.

There was to be one more twist. England were desperate to deny France the ball and embarked on a series of rolling mauls designed to eat up the clock. The tactic worked perfectly and when the drive was finally stopped, Andy Gomarsall hit Wilkinson with the ball and the fly-half cocked his left leg and hit a match-sealing drop goal. England had gone from complete no-hopers to World Cup finalists in just less than a month.

For Wilkinson, there were mixed feelings at full time. Although England had reached a second successive final, he could not shake off the disappointment at missing the conversion to Lewsey's try. That he also failed with a long-range first-half penalty attempt and a drop goal were further irritants to the self-proclaimed perfectionist and although his joy at reaching the final was evident, his furrowed brow also suggested there would be many painstaking hours spent on the training field during the week working on his kicking.

"It has been a funny story, this World Cup," he admitted. "Some of my kicks have gone over and some have not. But you just go back to it and give it all you have got. At the start some didn't go over and I realised I had to give it my all. It got better and they went over in the end. The fact that I get as many opportunities as I do is because the guys keep giving them to me. Every kick I miss they get me another one. With a bunch of guys like that you can't get disheartened.

"We have faced some incredible teams in this tournament – and none stronger than the one we have taken out tonight. That was an incredible performance by the French and I don't think my body has ever felt so sore. We have learned by going one game at a time. We have a day and an hour to really let it sink in. But don't fool yourselves for a second that the guys are not going to be thinking straightaway about going out and winning it next week."

Top: Jonny kicks the decisive drop goal against France in the semi-final.
Bottom: Jonny celebrates with Mike Catt after the final whistle has blown

For Ashton, victory was the perfect riposte to the critics who had written his team off before the tournament. England had made a mockery of all those who labelled them the worst defending champions in the history of the World Cup and Ashton now had the chance to emulate Sir Clive Woodward and lift the Webb Ellis trophy.

"We have some bright lads who have been through the mill and you can't buy experience like that," he said in his post-match press conference. "These guys won't give up. People talk about a British bulldog spirit and it is very much here in this group. We knew it was going to be tough tonight but we did think we had a side that could go out and beat France.

"We didn't actually get things right in the first half but we were a bit smarter in the second in terms of achieving field position. And we knew eventually we would get within sight of their posts and Jonny would kick them over."

All that stood between England, Wilkinson and another night of glory was South Africa.

England stood on the precipice of greatness as the World Cup final with the South Africans approached. No side had ever successfully defended their title in the 20-year-history of the competition and, after being written off as lambs to the slaughter, victory over the Springboks would rank as one of sport's greatest ever reversals in fortune.

England had emerged from their clash with the French relatively unscathed. Try scorer Josh Lewsey was ruled out with a hamstring injury but that aside, Ashton had a full squad to choose from and the only change to his starting XV was the recall of Mark Cueto for the unfortunate Wasps player.

The pre-match build-up was nothing if not intense. England were the underdogs but after their performances against Australia and France, the country was beginning to believe Wilkinson and the team could really do it. The 36–0 group stage drubbing by the South Africans had been an aberration and England were ready to put the record straight in Paris.

Unsurprisingly, Wilkinson was the centre of attention as the game approached. The talisman of the team, the slayer of the Wallabies and Les Bleus, the fly-half's every move was reported and analysed in minute detail but Wilkinson was unfazed. He was the same player he had been in 2003 and four years later, he admitted the big-match build-up still had exactly the same affect on him.

"I don't think I've ever played in a game when my heart wasn't racing," he said. "It's been like that since I was 18 but that's the life of a goal kicker for you. People might not think I look nervous, but the reality is different. I'm struggling to enjoy this occasion but I'm enjoying being here on this fantastic adventure with a fantastic group of players. Four years since the last World Cup has allowed me time to step out from the obsessive bubble I was in, take a broader view and get a little more control over my emotions.

"Then, when the Friday before a match comes round, I realise nothing much has changed. For instance, I won't leave the training ground until I'm perfectly happy with my kicking no matter how long it takes. You are desperate to do well for your team. That feeling doesn't change."

The day of the match finally arrived and when England took to the field at the Stade de France, Wilkinson did not betray any sign of nerves. The time had come for the talking to stop and England were 80 minutes away from making history.

The early exchanges were as fierce as everyone had predicted but it was the Springboks who struck first after six minutes. England inexplicably tried to run the ball out of their own 22 but Matthew Tait slipped, South African pounced and the young centre was penalised for holding onto the ball. Veteran full-back Percy Montgomery stepped forward and made no mistake with the simplest of penalty chances.

England however we back on terms just four minutes later courtesy of Wilkinson's unerring accuracy. Ashton's team moved the ball wide to Paul Sackey on the wing and South Africa killed the ball.

Wilkinson tries to breach the Springboks' tough defensive line

The penalty was almost on the touchline but Wilkinson took aim and his effort sailed through the uprights, making him the only player in the history of the game to score in two separate World Cup finals. South Africa stormed back into the lead when Montgomery landed his second penalty after 15 minutes and but the scorers were untroubled again until the stroke of half-time. With the Springboks laying siege to the England line, the first try of the match seemed inevitable but the men in white held and although they conceded a penalty that Montgomery converted for a 9–3 lead, Ashton's team appeared to have weathered the worst of the storm.

England came out for the second-half with determination etched on their faces and two minutes after the restart almost conjured up the try they craved. A superb break by Tait was stopped but Wilkinson spun the ball quickly to Cueto and the winger dived for the try line. Springbok number eight Danie Rossouw made a despairing tackle and referee Alain Rolland immediately went to the television match official to judge whether Ceuto's left foot had hit the touchline before the grounded the ball.

The decision seemed to take an eternity to come but when it finally did, it was heartbreak for England. The ruling was no try and although England already had a penalty for an earlier South African infringement, they had been denied five priceless points. Wilkinson took the three on offer but it was not enough.

The next score would be crucial and it went to the Springboks when Martin Corry was whistled and Montgomery duly landed his fourth penalty of the match. The lead was now 12–6 and when 20-year-old Francois Steyn kicked a long-range penalty on the hour mark, there was no way back for England. Wilkinson would get no further shots at goal to cut the arrears and however hard Ashton's team tried, they could find no way of unlocking the South African defence.

The final whistle confirmed the Springboks' 15–6 victory and as the South African players began their celebrations, Wilkinson and the rest of the England team began the painful process of coming to terms with their defeat. The ecstasy of victory in Sydney in 2003 had been replaced with agony in Paris.

"South Africa deserve to win, they've been fantastic all tournament so big respect to them," Wilkinson generously admitted after the game. "It's well due and it's their moment. But it's disappointing. We gave it everything. At times we got close enough and we never really felt we were going to lose.

"We had a lot of ground to catch up in this tournament and the guys all took the responsibility and I was proud of them all. It has been a hell of a journey. And we're proud of all the guys who've gone out of their way to support us."

England had come so close to providing a fairytale ending to their World Cup story but despite the bitter disappointment of losing in the final, there was still much to be proud of in the wake of their dramatic improvement over the course of the tournament.

"They did fantastically well getting into the final but in days to come, they'll reflect on what they've done and be really proud," Ashton said in Paris. "I thought they rose to the occasion absolutely magnificently. I don't think anyone outside the squad gave them a cat in hell's chance of doing anything at all, but they were right in the game until the final whistle. South Africa have been the form team in the tournament, there's no doubt about that. Over the seven weeks, I think they deserve to win."

Whether Wilkinson's World Cup story has another chapter to be written remains to be seen. The fly-half will only be 32 years' old when the next World Cup – being staged in New Zealand in 2011 – is upon us. If Jonny can avoid the injury bug that blighted him from 2004–07, few would bet against him being there to spearhead England's bid to reclaim the Webb Ellis Trophy. His dedication, sheer will to win and competitive spirit will not be dimmed by a four-year wait to play in a fourth World Cup and England's challenge will only be strengthened by his presence.

Opposite: South Africa prove too tough to break down in the final.
Overleaf: Jonny walks off the stage after collecting his silver medal

iRB
RUGBY
WORLD CUP
2007

Fran

iRB
RUGBY
WORLD CUP
2007

THE STORY SO FAR...

Name: Jonny Peter Wilkinson
Born: 25 May 1979, Frimley
Position: Fly-half
Height: 5ft 10in (1.77m)
Weight: 13st 5lbs

INTERNATIONAL CAREER
Country: England
Debut: 4 April 1998 v Ireland
Caps: 65
Test Points: 1,029
Test Tries: 7
Penalties: 207
Conversions: 146
Drop Goals: 27

CLUB CAREER
Club: Newcastle Falcons
League Appearances: 126
Total Points: 1,363
Tries: 23
Penalties: 274
Conversions: 183
Drop Goals: 20

Statistics correct as at 22 October 2007